How to sell Industry 4.0 to Central and Eastern Europe

Internationalisation strategies for Czech Republic, Poland, Romania, Hungary, Bulgaria, Slovenia, Slovakia and Lithuania

by Richard Eichele

Content, cover design and illustrations (unless otherwise marked in the text) by:

Richard Eichele
Eichenallee 11
32791 Lage
Germany

ISBN: 979-8-6712-9519-1

The Agenda

Chapter 1 - Prologue

For companies from the most diverse countries and industries, growth by increasing sales is one of the most important factors when it comes to corporate success.[1] However, in times of steadily increasing competition between companies in and saturation on home markets, it is a difficult undertaking to

---

[1] Cf. C.K. Prahalad and Venkat Ramaswamy (2004, 5).

achieve the desired growth year after year. In order to withstand this growth pressure, the expansion of business activities to foreign markets seems unavoidable for many companies.[2] This is also quickly apparent when looking at the development of the global export volume.

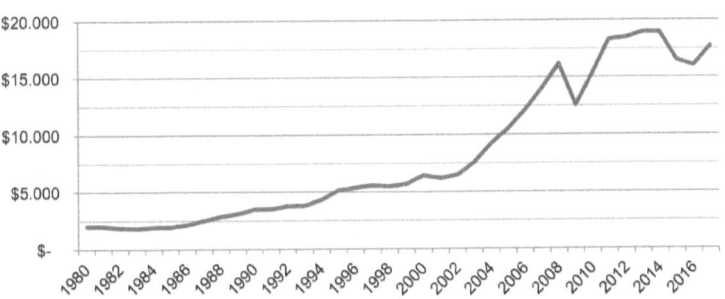

Figure 1.1: Worldwide Export value in billion US Dollar per year[3]

In 1980, for example, only USD 2,036 billion worth of goods were exported worldwide. By opening

[2] Cf. Berndt, Fantapié Altobelli and Sander (3).

[3] Cf. World Trade Organization (2019).

borders and concluding trade agreements, the internationalisation of companies has progressed. It is therefore not surprising that export volumes have risen to USD 17,730 billion by 2017. This increase clearly shows how important international trade is for companies. However, in order to be able to make a well-founded decision about an expansion and a market entry into new countries, there are some factors that have to be analysed beforehand. These include, for example, questions regarding local conditions or the current competitive situation in the target country.[4]

The aim of this elaboration is the well-founded definition of a market entry strategy for countries in Central and Eastern Europe, which is one of the most important markets for the world of industrial automation.

---

[4] Cf. Koch (2017, 66ff.).

First, an overview of the general problem of internationalisation of companies and a short introduction of the economic framework and the competitive situation in Central and Eastern Europe will take place.

Subsequently, methods for classifying target markets into market typologies will be presented on the basis of market attractiveness and market barrier criteria.

In the last sections of this elaboration these methods will be used, extended and supported by empirical data. After that, an internationalisation approach is determined from the market typologies of all countries in Central and Eastern Europe as the result of this elaboration.

Chapter 2 - How international your company really is

„The theory of games shows how coalitions should be formed if there is an advantage in forming them and the rules do not forbid it. Any player, in fact, who fails to attempt a coalition in such circumstances will lose or, more exactly, will gain less. The rational player must make the pessimistic assumption that a coalition may be formed against him; and he must therefore attempt to form one himself."[5]

---

[5] McDonald (1996).

The foreign trade policy of states or communities of states is generally based on a model that has an influence on the structure of international trade relations. These models can be e.g. "Free Trade" and "Protectionism". While a history of foreclosure to other countries has often been viewed as positive, markets have clearly liberalised in recent years. Today, with 164 members since 29 July 2016, including European countries, the WTO deals with global rules of trade between nations to smoothen international free trade.[6] The objectives of the WTO are the greatest possible transparency of the trade policies of its members, the agreement, observance and monitoring of the common multilateral trade rules and the ongoing liberalisation of world trade, which should ultimately lead to the strengthening of economic stability and

[6] Cf. World Trade Organization (2019).

competitiveness. The special development interests of the poorer and poorest members will be given special consideration.[7]

Figure 2.1: International trade in goods of the euro area[8]

The European domestic market has now been in existence for over 25 years and is more successful than ever before.[9] The European Union with the exports of goods to the rest of the world of 183.3

[7] Cf. Peter Altmaier (24.09.2018).

[8] Baiba Grandovska and Michele Marotta (Februar 2019, 1).

[9] Cf. European Commission (2019, 7).

billion Euro in February 2019 is one of the most outward-looking economies in the world (cf. figure 2.1). It also is the world's largest domestic market. Free trade between its Member States has been one of the basic principles in the construction of the EU, opening world trade is also an important objective of the Union.[10] By promoting research, innovation and technological progress, the EU is an attractive and important location for technically oriented companies. Projects such as "Horizon Europa" are expected to provide 100 billion Euro for research and innovation by 2027.[11]

---

[10] Cf. Baiba Grandovska and Michele Marotta (Februar 2019, 1f.).

[11] Cf. European Commission (2019, 17ff.).

The degree of internationalisation of a company

A company is considered to be international if its activities abroad are essential to achieving and securing its corporate goals.[12] In the literature different considerations are cited for the measurement of the extent of the international activity of an enterprise, of which the quantitative and not the qualitative is explained here.

If international companies are not included on the basis of quantitative

key figures, both non-cumulative values, that is, time-related characteristics, and relative characteristics that each refer to a specific period are considered.

---

[12] Cf. Perlitz and Schrank (2013, 12).

Table 2.1: Examples for non-cumulative values and movement quantities[13]

Non-cumulative values	Movement quantities
Number of countries in which the company is active	Foreign sales
Number of foreign branches	Incoming orders from abroad
Assets abroad	foreign profit
Number of persons employed abroad	
Number of foreign members in top management	
foreign investment	

One of the most important relative variables is the foreign ratio, which can be formed for each of the quantitative values, for example, by relating them to the domestic value or the value for the international acting company as a whole.

[13] Cf. Lutz Sommer (2009, 95).

Mathematically, one of the quantitative-absolute values mentioned above is related to the domestic value or the value of the international acting company as a whole. For example, it is possible to look at foreign sales in relation to total sales or to compare the proportion of employees employed abroad with the number of employees in the company as a whole in order to make statements about the significance of the foreign sales in relation to the total sales.[14]

---

[14] Cf. Kutschker (2011, 259ff.)

Table 2.2: Common foreign quota calculations[15]

Foreign quota	Calculation
Foreign sales compared to the total turnover	$$\frac{Foreign\,sales}{Total\,turnover}$$
Foreign quota of employees	$$\frac{Employees\,in\,foreign\,country}{Total\,employees\,in\,global\,company\,group}$$
Foreign quota in executive boards	$$\frac{Number\,of\,chief\,officers\,coming\,from\,the\,headquarters}{Number\,of\,chief\,officers\,in\,foreign\,country}$$

The various foreign quotas of a company can be clearly presented in an internationalisation profile. This profile shows very clearly the extent to which a global acting company is internationalising with regard to different characteristics.[16]

In addition to company-related parameters, it is also possible to include market and competition-related considerations of a whole country.

---

[15] Cf. SIMON-KUCHER & PARNTER (2005, 5).

[16] Cf. Lutz Sommer (2009, 97).

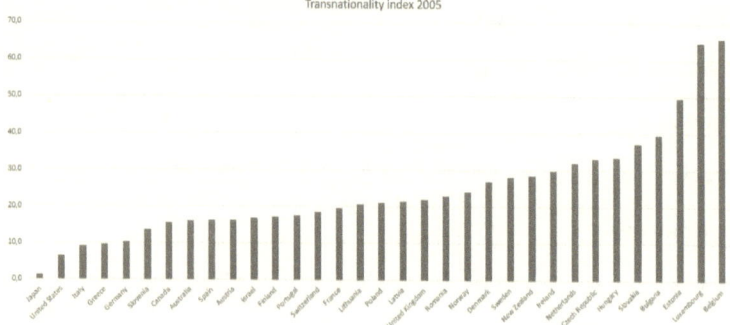

Transnationality index 2005

Figure 2.2: Transnationality Index 2005[17]

The United Nations Conference on Trade and Development (UNCTAD) measures internationality of a whole country using the Transnationality Index. This indicator covers the individual indicators of wealth abroad, turnover abroad and employees abroad, with each individual indicator having its own weighting.[18] Figure 2.2 shows that Germany has

---

[17] UNCTAD (23.09.2008).

[18] Cf. UNCTAD (2019).

got a low value in the transnationality index compared to other European states. This is an indicator for the importance of internationalisation especially for German companies.

The importance of internationalisation

Globalisation, for all its flaws and mismanagement, has benefited the world and has been advancing technology by leaps.[19]

An internationalisation strategy as a step in the direction of globalisation describes the sum of decisions to expand value-added activities beyond the national borders of a country, whereby the creation and maintenance of success potentials is the primary goal.

It includes the development of concrete action targets such as the definition of a market entry strategy in future markets as well as the definition of consistent activities and resource allocations to

---

[19] Cf. Moak (2017, 247).

ensure the highest possible degree of achievement of the fundamental, long-term corporate goals.[20]

At the level of overall company strategies, it is up to the company management to decide whether and on which markets the company is to operate. The questions to be answered by the company prior to internationalisation are the following:

1. should the company take the step abroad at all? What are the motives for this? What goals are being pursued?

2. which countries/regions can be considered for internationalisation?

3. what form should international involvement take? Is a national company or a representative office sought?

---

[20] Cf. Ernst (1999, 83f.).

Making the fundamental decision for or against internationalisation

The decision-making process for internationally oriented companies lays down three conditions that must apply simultaneously in order to make direct investments abroad (FDI) by a company worthwhile. [21]

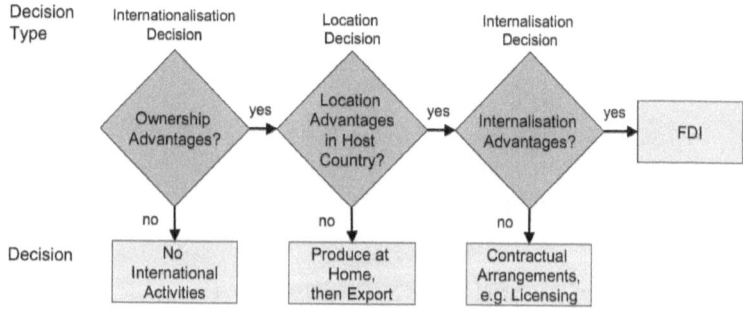

Figure 2.3: The OLI Decision Process for Foreign Operation Modes[22]

---

[21] Cf. Dunning and Lundan (2008, 96ff.).

[22] Welch, Benito and Petersen (2007, 31); Sudarsanam (2009, 201).

1. Owner-specific advantages (O): the company must have some unique competitive advantages (firm specific advantages, FSA) that outweigh the disadvantages of competing with local companies in their home market. Often, these advantages result from the ownership of intangible assets that are (at least temporarily) company-specific.

2. Location-specific advantages (L): If foreign direct investment is to be made, it must be more profitable for the company to operate abroad than in its home country. Otherwise, foreign markets would be served by other means. Site-specific advantages (or country-specific advantages, CSAs) can be, for example, labor costs, efficient and skilled labor, customs duties, transport costs or natural resources.

3. Advantages of internalisation (I): companies that have specific advantages can either use them themselves (internalise them) or sell them to other companies.[23]

With the help of the OLI decision-making process, a fundamental decision on internationalisation can be brought about.

The decision-making process, whether internationalisation should be part of the company's strategy or not, will not be further developed within the framework of this elaboration. Furthermore, it is assumed in the following that a fundamental decision on internationalisation has already taken place in the company and that the determination of the internationalisation goals is of much greater importance.

---

[23] Cf. Dunning and Lundan (2008, 96ff.).

Why internationalisation brings advantages to a company

Due to the influence of international organisations, as described in the previous chapter, there are various examples of internationalisation incentives.

Table 2.3: Examples of internationalisation incentives[24]

Internationalisation incentive	Example
Subsidies	Export subsidies or subsidies for setting up production facilities abroad serve either the domestic economy or other policy objectives, e.g. in connection with development aid. Export subsidies include export premiums, transport subsidies and export credits with favorable interest and repayment terms.
Tax advantages	Tax advantages include tax-free reserves or the deductibility of losses of foreign subsidiaries and double taxation agreements.
Takeover of infrastructure measures	Railway connections, ship road extension
Consultation	Essential information and services can be obtained from the Chambers of Foreign Trade and the Federal Agency for Foreign Trade for free.

---

[24] Cf. Wiesner (2005, 69ff.).

Economic framework of industrial countries in Central and Eastern Europe

Unfettered trade and global investments, which are the original drivers of globalisation, did enhance global economic growth because taking advantage of comparative advantage brought economies of scale.[25] One of the most important regions in the world for the ongoing development of a globalised industrial economy is the eight Central and Eastern European Countries (CEEC8) that have joined the EU in the early 2000s. The CEEC8 countries are Bulgaria, Czech Republic, Hungary, Lithuania, Poland, Romania, Slovakia and Slovenia. By 2017 these eight countries were home to 98 million people with a combined GDP of US$ 2,7 trillion.[26]

---

[25] Cf. Moak (2017, 225).

[26] Cf. IZA Institute of Labor Economics (2019, 2).

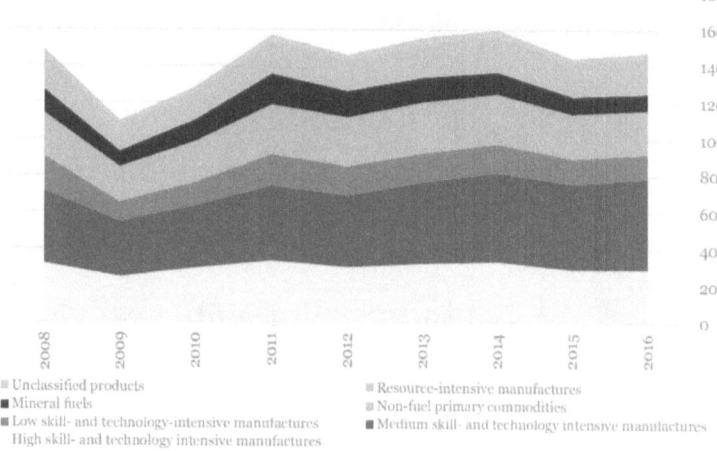

Billions US$ (Constant 2000)

- Unclassified products
- Mineral fuels
- Low skill- and technology-intensive manufactures
  High skill- and technology intensive manufactures
- Resource-intensive manufactures
- Non-fuel primary commodities
- Medium skill- and technology intensive manufactures

Figure 2.4: Export skills of the CEEC8 countries[27]

Summing up the exported goods of the CEEC8 countries a high amount of resource-intensive manufactures is exported in the world market. Especially a rising trend in the exports of technology intensive manufactures up to around 50 billion US$ in 2016 can be noticed with a rising trend (compare from figure 2.2).

---

[27] IZA Institute of Labor Economics (2019, 13).

The target countries for German exports of industrial automation, which include Central and Eastern Europe, are diverse. The Central Eastern European countries, which are very advanced in their economic development, are not only sales markets for German companies anymore or extended workbenches, but partners at eye level. Together with them, Germany is taking major steps towards industry 4.0. In Poland alone, over 10 billion euros from the "Intelligent Development" program will be available by 2020. Latvia and Lithuania were among the EU countries with the highest growth in innovators in 2016. As part of the Eastern Europe Business Day 2017, which also deals with the topic of digitisation/industry 4.0, many innovative projects with and in Eastern Europe that prove why the region is so attractive for German companies will be shown.[28]

---

[28] Cf. GTAI (2017, 5).

Chapter 3 - Assessment of market typologies and determination of an internationalisation strategy

When does one speak of an international company?

How is this determined?

The literature contains a large number of definitions and there is no uniform definition of the term international enterprise. If one follows the institutional approach, then a company is considered international if it carries out activities abroad. However, the question of the degree of foreign involvement above which a company can be regarded as international is important. Despite many different measurement concepts for assessing the degree of internationalisation, there is no clear definition.[29]

An internationally oriented company with many international locations creates its benefit by maintaining a monopolistic advantage and avoiding or restricting competition. Some authors criticise this view and argue that it does not sufficiently explain how business benefits are generated at all (i.e. focusing only on "unfair" cross-border exploitation rather than welfare enhancing creation of benefits) and ignores the fact that internationally

---

[29] Cf. Kutschker (2011, 246ff.).

oriented companies are potentially better able to conduct cross-border activities internally than independent companies. It should be noted that internationally oriented companies tend to be more competitive than nationally oriented companies.[30]

Figure 3.1: The failed merger of Daimler Chrysler[31]

The man was too impudent. He had his own opinion: Unfortunately, the wrong one.[32]

---

[30] Cf. Stephen Herbert Hymer (June, 1960, 1ff.).

[31] Büschemann (07.05.2013).

[32] Cf. Büschemann (07.05.2013).

On May 7, 1998, the companies Daimler, personified by Jürgen Schrempp and Chrysler with Bob Eaton in London for one of the most innovative mergers of the automotive industry before the media. The merger already burst in 2007 - the reasons are manifold and are proof that even international investments on a large scale can fail due to corporate cultural reasons.[33]

This chapter explains approaches and theoretical tools that can be used to make decisions about an internationalisation strategy with the help of market typologies, diverse internationalisation models and a main focus in the national culture. With the different tools shown in this chapter a list of criteria will be created in the next chapter to evaluate the right internationalisation strategy.

---

[33] Cf. Büschemann (07.05.2013).

Analysis of country market typologies

Internationalisation does not work suddenly but slowly and gradually. The process of internationalisation is not only the result of long-term strategies, but also of successive decisions that are adapted from time to time. Only after time and the approval of all decision makers in the company can companies be transformed into international corporate groups that can use all the competitive advantages mentioned above.[34]

Once a company has made the fundamental decision for internationalisation, it must first examine, within the framework of a market selection process, to what extent the market(s) envisaged offer good chances of success for its motives for internationalisation and whether the risk of becoming active in the country

---

[34] Cf. Swoboda (2002, 72f.).

or several countries is justifiable. Both, location approaches and Porter's diamond approach, reflect criteria on the basis of which a country market can be specified.

What is a market?

The term market is a term that is difficult to define because there are many different ways of looking at it. Economic theory describes the classical market as the place where companies exchange goods with potential customers. Customers usually only participate in the exchange of goods on the market. The rest of the time they are rather passive, and the companies try to design, produce or market the goods on their own.[35] Nowadays the market deals with many more participants. These include competitors, buyers and suppliers of a company. Building on this, it can also be further subdivided. If one refers e.g. to suppliers one speaks of the procurement market. If one only considers the demand side, i.e. the customers, the

---

[35] Cf. C.K. Prahalad and Venkat Ramaswamy (2004, 6).

sales market is meant.[36] In addition, institutions such as supervisory boards, authorities or other stakeholders (the public) can also influence the company. Accordingly, the market represents the microeconomic environment and thus influences the activities of a company. This also happens in the opposite direction, because the company can also influence the microeconomic environment and the markets and interest groups it contains. There are also macroeconomic factors. These only influence the market indirectly but have a considerable influence on a company. Macroeconomic influences include, for example, political, legal, economic, technological, ecological or socio-cultural factors or decisions that influence them.[37] Enterprises can hardly influence the macroeconomic environment at all, as they are more or less given.

---

[36] Cf. Bea and Haas (2017, 101).

[37] Cf. Meffert, Burmann and Kirchgeorg (2015, 43f.).

The right way for a market analysis

The market analysis is intended to clarify to companies which opportunities and risks are hidden in the markets and thus has the goal of determining the market attractiveness, market potentials and opportunities in the market. On the one hand, the demand and supply sides with their activities and strategies are analysed in terms of type, strength and direction. These can usually be influenced by the company and thus determine the controllable success of the company. In addition, however, factors of the macroeconomic environment must also be considered in the market analysis, as these also influence market success or market attractive-ness.[38] Central questions in the market analysis are for example:

---

[38] Cf. Grunwald and Hempelmann (2017, 142).

- *What is the size of the market in terms of sales volume and number of customers?*

- *What framework conditions does the market offer with regard to politics or society?*

- *Which customers, vendors or competitors still participate in the market and how do they do this?*[39]

In order to answer these questions, the relevant market must first be defined in order to clearly define the scope of the investigation. After that, various market analysis instruments can be used.[40]

These include, for example, market segmentation, environmental analysis, competitor analysis or buyer analysis. Due to the internationalisation of companies and activities on foreign markets, cultural differences do play an increasingly important role,

---

[39] Cf. Biesel (2013, 53f.).

[40] Cf. Grunwald and Hempelmann (2017, 143).

which has led to an analysis of these factors in the market analysis.[41] For data collection, primary market research data can be collected as well as secondary data. The latter is information that has already been collected in the past. The advantage is that they are easier to access and often freely available. For example, there are publications by domestic and foreign authorities, institutes and industry associations. Subsidiaries often also have market-relevant reports or information. A disadvantage of this is that these data are often not up-to-date or inaccurate. Primary research, on the other hand, is prepared for a specific purpose and thus provides exactly the data you want to receive. It is rarely used as it is usually carried out by market research institutes and presupposes a considerable cost and time expenditure.[42]

---

[41] Cf. Kutschker (2011, 671f.).

[42] Cf. Koch (2017, 225ff.).

Analysis of market typologies with market attractiveness and market barriers

Within the framework of the selection and prioritisation of country markets, the aim is on the one hand to describe the attractiveness of the targeted country markets in order to find out which opportunities the country markets bring with them. In addition, the question of which of the competitive advantages existing in the home country can also be exploited internationally should also be addressed. On the other hand, the market barriers that have to be overcome in order to gain access to the markets have to be identified. Here language barriers or even state restrictions can be of importance or whether the market is already occupied by a very strong national supplier.

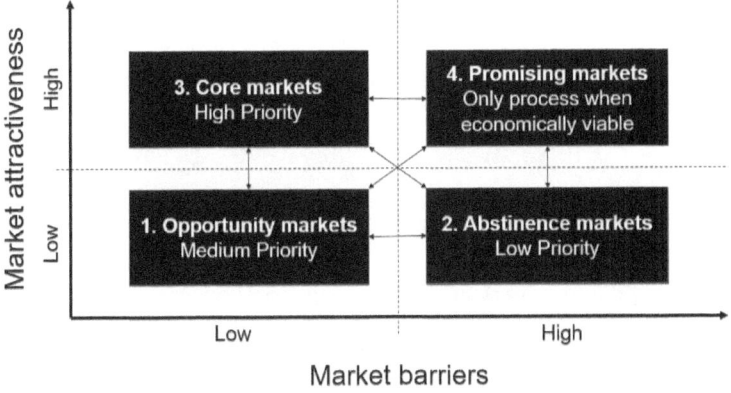

Figure 3.2: Country market typologies[43]

The objective of the market selection process is thus to use the criteria of market attractiveness and market barriers to find out which country markets in general, which country markets at some point in the future, which markets occasionally, and which markets should not be worked on at all.

---

[43] Own illustration by the author according to Backhaus and Voeth (2010, 71).

1. **Opportunity markets**

   Medium priority should be given to those country markets that have a low market attractiveness and hardly any market barriers. These markets are referred to as occasional markets.

2. **Abstinence markets**

   Abstinence markets are characterized by high market barriers but very low market attractiveness. Abstinence markets should only be dealt with very low priority or not at all.

3. **Core markets**

   The highest priority should be given to opening up country markets that are both highly attractive and easily accessible.

4. Promising markets

If it is considered economically viable to work this market, this market should also be prioritised accordingly.

Porter's diamond approach

Porter's starting point with his diamond approach is the empirical observation that many globally successful companies come from one and the same industry in one country. Over several years, Porter and his research team have investigated the competitive advantages of companies in different countries in Europe, Asia and America. These studies have shown that competitive advantages within a nation are sector-specific. Not one nation but certain sectors of a nation are globally competitive. Thus, it is not possible to speak of the competitiveness of a country, but it is always a question of how the environmental conditions for companies in individual sectors within the country are structured in order to achieve the highest possible productivity - and thus also international competitiveness - in competition with one another. Porter therefore does not look at the country level, but at the branch or company level.[44]

According to Porter, there are good and bad environmental conditions in a country for the promotion of competition between companies. The international competitiveness of an industry therefore depends on four main and two secondary elements of the overall economy, which Porter combines into the Porter diamond. These elements determine whether knowledge and skills develop faster in a country than elsewhere, whether information is disseminated better and whether product ideas and process optimisations are implemented more quickly.[45]

---

[44] Cf. Kutschker (2011, 447); Cf. Michael E. Porter (1990, 76f.).

[45] Cf. Cynthia A. Montgomery and Michael E. Porter (1991, 151).

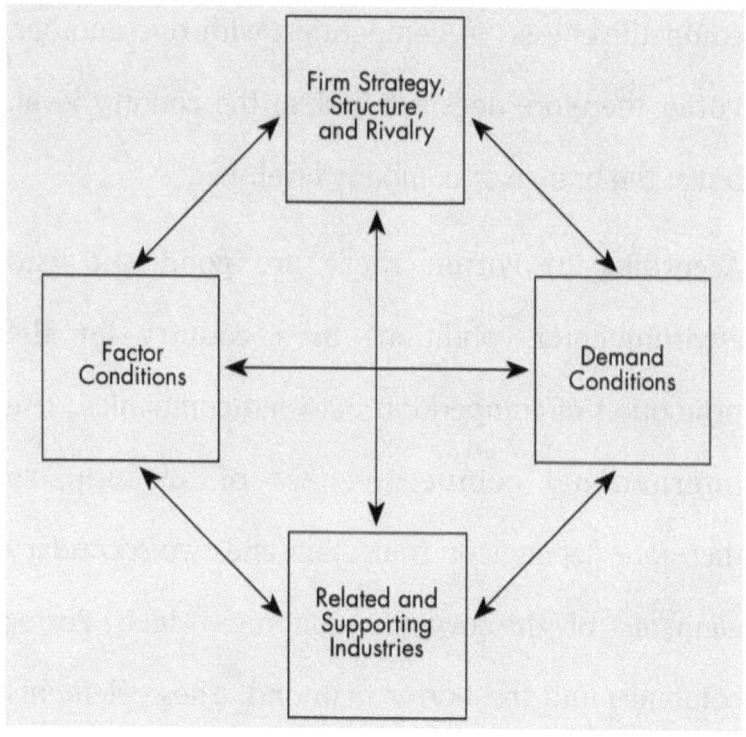

Figure 3.3: Determinants of National Competitive Advantage[46]

Porter graphically arranges the elements of nations' competitive advantage to create a diamond, from which the name Porter diamond is derived.

[46] Michael E. Porter (1990, 78).

The main influencing factors, which can be found in the picture above, are:

1. Firm Strategy, Structure and Rivalry,

2. Factor Conditions,

3. Demand Conditions and

4. Related and Supporting industries.[47]

Further influencing factors that are reflected in modified graphics and also influence competitive advantages are:

5. The state and

6. Coincidence.[48]

According to Porter, those countries in which the individual elements of the diamond reinforce each other positively possess long-term national competitive advantages. In his opinion, no country

---

[47] Cf. Michael E. Porter (1990, 78).

[48] Cf. Kutschker (2011, 449).

can be internationally competitive in all industries. In this respect, the decision to internationalise a company must be preceded by a precise analysis of the international competition in its sector via the diamond.[49]

While the location approaches focus primarily on the goal of internationalisation, Porter points out the origin of internationalisation. He does not speak about the competitiveness of a whole economy but of the result of a country's competitive industries. Accordingly, in his country analysis he looks at those factors that make industries internationally competitive. Only countries that have a well-functioning diamond in an industry, i.e. a good interaction of the six diamond factors, have long-

---

[49] Cf. Michael E. Porter (1990, 76ff.).

term national competitive advantages and are also internationally competitive in this industry.[50]

In the following sections the four or six elements of the diamond are explained in detail.

Firm strategy, Structure and Rivalry

Decisive for the competitive advantages of nations are the corporate strategies and structures and the rivalry of the companies located there. Here, Porter looks at how industries and companies have formed in the respective countries and how they are organised and managed. The advantages in international competition are therefore particularly felt by those companies that are managed according to long-term goals.

In addition to internal company strategies and structures, the number of competing companies and the intensity of competition in an industry are

---

[50] Cf. Kutschker (2011, 447f.).

particularly important: strong competition on domestic markets is a strong incentive for the durability of competitive advantages. An enterprise benefits from strong domestic competition between enterprises in the same sector. The positive effects on competitiveness result from innovation competition within the domestic industry.[51]

Factor conditions

Factor conditions are the equipment of a country with the production factors labor, land and capital, not only quantity and quality, but also the various possibilities to combine them. Factors include in particular human capital, investment capital, infrastructure, information and communication networks and natural resources. Of particular interest is the ability to combine production factors to create innovation.

---

[51] Cf. Michael E. Porter (1990, 78f.).

According to Porter, the competitive advantage of a company is greatest in a country when that country has all the factors needed to compete in its particular industry, such as automation. In contrast to previous explanatory approaches, which considered the availability of natural resources to be a particularly important factor, Porter takes a more critical view of a country's natural resource base. Consequently, the availability of natural resources can also have a negative impact on a company's efforts in international competition. In his opinion, the compulsion to replace non-existent natural resources with other factors leads to greater innovation and thus to greater competitiveness.[52]

Demand conditions

All factors that have an influence on demand fall under demand conditions. This refers to customers'

---

[52] Cf. Perlitz and Schrank (2013, 96); Michael E. Porter (1990, 78f.).

expectations of the quality of products and services as well as market size and growth. Demanding and difficult domestic buyers with regard to products and services lead to competitive advantages in these sectors abroad, as they exert permanent pressure on companies to innovate, forcing them to develop further and thus become more competitive.

The size and growth of the domestic market can also be a competitive advantage. Especially in industries in which R&D, economies of scale and learning effects play a major role, a positive competitive effect is created by the need to invest in new products and services to amortise quickly.[53]

Related and supporting industries

Porter assumes that an internationally successful company also needs internationally successful suppliers.

---

[53] Cf. Michael E. Porter (1990, 78f.).

Supply industries play an important role primarily because of the efficient supply of the necessary inputs, but also in order to generate product and process improvements through close cooperation. One example of the so-called supply chain approach is the automotive industry, where product quality and innovation of production parts as well as the interaction between suppliers and manufacturers in connection with just-in-time production and distinctive quality management throughout all stages of the process chain play a very important role. Only if the suppliers themselves also use global advantages can they be good partners for the company as a global player in international competition.[54]

The state

In addition to the four main influencing factors, Porter cites the state as a secondary element. The

---

[54] Cf. Michael E. Porter (1990, 78f.).

state can influence the four core elements and change them both positively and negatively. Through legislation, subsidies, guarantees or its own demand, it can either promote or hinder national competitive advantages. For example, a rigorous implementation of anti-trust provisions in a country can lead to an intensified competitive situation and thus trigger innovations through the competition between companies, which then lead to national competitive advantages. Another example would be state investment in education or infrastructure in order to sustainably support competitiveness.[55]

Coincidence

Random events also play a major role in the development of the competitiveness of an industry. As examples of such random events, Porter cites random discoveries, major technological break-

---

[55] Cf. Perlitz and Schrank (2013, 100).

throughs, fluctuations in the prices of means of production, significant cuts in the capital markets and political or military conflicts. For example, the high rise in American wages and salaries in the early post-war years led to increased automation to compensate for these labor cost disadvantages.[56]

---

[56] Cf. Perlitz and Schrank (2013, 99f.).

Scoring procedures to determine market attractiveness and market barriers

With its diamond approach, Porter merely provides a qualitative overview of the requirements for founding an international company with competitive advantages. [57] In order to determine market attractiveness and market barriers, quantitative data is required that can be used to compare different markets. Porter's diamond approach alone is not sufficient for the comparable determination of these criteria. As the allocation of country markets can change over time as a result of changes in the attractiveness of the market for the company or as a result of changes in market barriers, the assessment should be repeated at regular intervals on the basis

---

[57] Cf. Kutschker (2011, 449).

of the above criteria. Also, therefore quantified data is necessary.

The scoring procedure is a methodology that is intended to provide rational support for decision-making on complex problems. The scoring method is a relatively old method that has its origins in economic utility analysis. The scoring procedure is also used in controlling, in project management, in economics and even in public procurement law, wherever an assessment has to be made on the basis of several quantitative and qualitative criteria, goals or conditions.[58]

The central analysis step when processing the scoring procedure is the weighting of the previously defined selection criteria. The weighting factors indicate the importance of the individual criteria. The weightings are purely subjective. The decision

---

[58] Cf. Westermann and Finger (2012).

maker determines what is important and what is not. In order for the scoring procedure and the decision-making process to remain transparent, the weightings should be methodical.[59]

For the evaluation of criteria, uniform scales are typically used, which usually have five to ten numeric or verbal states of expression (e.g. from "very good" to "very bad"). With regard to the number of states of expression, an even number is particularly recommended in order to force positioning within the states of expression and to eliminate the "urge to the center". The individual characteristics of an object are evaluated by specifying probabilities for all scale values. The sum of the scale values multiplied by the respective probabilities gives the expected value of each criterion. These are now multiplied by a weighting

---

[59] Cf. Zardari et al. (2015).

factor that expresses the significance of the individual criterion. The sum of the weighting factors for all factors is 1 (linear weighting). The overall assessment value of the object is therefore the sum of the weighted expected values for all characteristics.[60]

In order to evaluate the criteria explained in the following part of this section, the scoring procedure will be applied in the fourth section.

[60] Cf. Helm (2009, 217ff.).

Chapter 4 - Assignment of the country market attractiveness

In order to decide on the attractiveness of a country market, it is examined which economic success factors open up special opportunities for the company in the respective country market. Central opportunities for the company in the potential countries result from these categories of advantages:[61]

---

[61] Cf. Backhaus (2003, 127).

Production cost advantages

Production cost advantages can arise from e.g. lower labor costs, longer working hours, longer machine running times, an improvement in the utilisation of production capacities or procurement advantages through better supply of raw materials as well as more favourable prices for raw materials and materials.

Demand-related advantages

Sales-related advantages are the result, for example, from the increased number of potential customers due to market development (market volume), market structure and market growth (securing future markets), country-specific purchasing power and, if necessary, price sensitivity of the buyer groups.

Competitive advantages

Competitive advantages can result, for example, from technological superiority as well as from the intensity of competition (e.g. judged on the basis of Porter's diamond). Here, the number, power and strategic orientation of competitors (defensive/offensive) are analysed. In addition to the market shares of the leading competitors, their financial strength and other resources must also be included in the analysis. In addition to direct market attractiveness, indirect attractiveness is often just as important.

The point here is to consider the country's opportunities in combination with other countries. In order to examine how the existing suppliers "defend themselves" against a new competitor, the following 4 elements have to be considered[62] :

Advantages/disadvantages of size:

Here it has to be examined whether you as a new supplier have economies of scale or disadvantages compared to your established competitors. In addition, the industry structure is generally interesting here. If there are only a few, but significant suppliers, the danger of a price war is great.

Bottleneck factors:

It is also necessary to look at competitors who can hinder the new company by keeping important suppliers away from them or blocking necessary sales channels. This can happen, for example, if a new supplier of automation technology is not listened to by local system integrators, as they have

---

[62] Cf. Backhaus and Voeth (2010, 85ff.).

already been supplied with framework agreements by local suppliers[63]. Thus, if the resident companies have a broad and closed product range, these combined effects can make it more difficult for the new company to gain access to the market.

Irreversibility:

How difficult it would be for a company to reverse the investment is also important. The higher the exit barriers due to high investment sums e.g. in production buildings and machines, long-term contracts or state rules prohibiting redundancies, the harder the competitor will act against new competitors.

Conditions of competition (regulated by the state):

If there are legal rules to regulate competitive conditions, these should be considered. Are there such authorities and how active are they? The more

---

[63] Own example by the author

regulated the market, the more difficult it is to enter it.

Internalisation advantages:

Here it is necessary to analyse which advantages arise with regard to the optimisation of logistics due to internationalisation. In addition, an analysis of the supply of skilled workers also plays a role.

Digital competitive factors

The IMD World Digital Competitiveness ranking analyses and ranks countries' ability to adopt and explore digital technologies. Based on the research, the methodology of the World Digital Competitiveness ranking defines digital competitiveness into three main factors:

1. Knowledge

2. Technology

3. Future-readiness.

Each of these factors is divided into 3 sub-factors which describe every facet of the areas analysed. Each sub-factor has the same weight in the overall consolidation of results.[64]

---

[64] Cf. IMD WORLD COMPETITIVENESS CENTER (2018, 28).

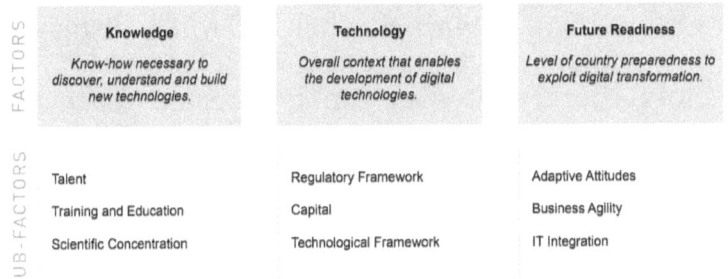

Figure 4.1: Digital Competitiveness Factors and Sub-factors[65]

Knowledge is one of the selected criteria because it is necessary to discover, understand and build new technologies.[66] The factor technology concludes the overall context that enables the development of digital technologies in general.[67] The third factor future readiness includes the level of country preparedness to take advantage of digital

---

[65] IMD WORLD COMPETITIVENESS CENTER (2018, 29).

[66] Cf. IMD WORLD COMPETITIVENESS CENTER (2018, 36).

[67] Cf. IMD WORLD COMPETITIVENESS CENTER (2018, 37).

transformation.[68] With the help of these displayed factors country profiles can be created for every country in the world.

The data collection is consisting of statistics from international regional and national sources and an international panel of expert's executive opinion surveys.[69]

---

[68] Cf. IMD WORLD COMPETITIVENESS CENTER (2018, 38).

[69] Cf. IMD WORLD COMPETITIVENESS CENTER (2018, 29).

Chapter 5 - Assignment of the country market barriers

"Governments are very creative when it comes to the invention or virtuous use of non-tariff barriers to protect their countries' industries from international competition"[70]

---

[70] Mühlbacher, Leihs and Dahringer (2006, 147).

The term "market barriers" covers a large number of obstacles to mobility which make it difficult or even impossible to enter or exit a market. The existence of market barriers is of equal economic and business significance. From an economic point of view, they influence the functioning and outcome of the competitive process.[71]

Market barriers can be categorised in different ways.

[71] Cf. Bain (1956); Weizsäcker (1980, 6ff.).

Tariff barriers

First, the country itself offers the possibility of introducing market barriers through tariff barriers.

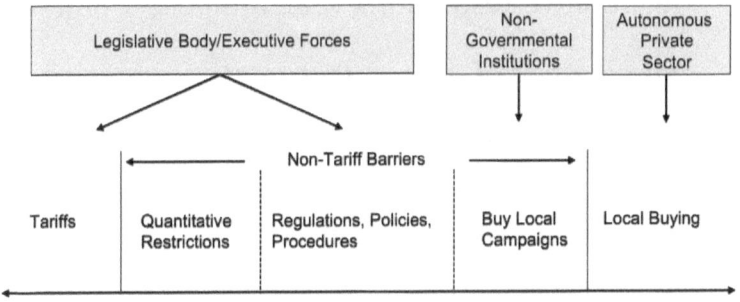

Figure 5.1: Categories of trade barriers[72]

Customs duties and taxes on certain internationally traded goods have traditionally been used to protect the internal market. The import of goods, for example, is artificially made more difficult in order to make the purchase of goods produced on the

---

[72] Morschett, Schramm-Klein and Zentes (2015, 151).

internal market more attractive. However, due to the liberalisation of world trade (see Chapter 2 of this paper), states are increasingly inventing barriers other than tariffs and taxes. Examples for non-tariff-barriers are: [73]

- quantitative restrictions which impose a limit on the quantity of a good that may be exported or imported in or from a country

- laws, regulations, policies or procedures in general that impede international trade between foreign countries

- "buy local" campaigns (e.g. "America first" campaign)

In addition to permanent tariff and non-tariff barriers, international trade is also influenced by temporary barriers. These can be imposed due to reactions to certain events in intergovernmental

---

[73] Cf. Morschett, Schramm-Klein and Zentes (2015, 151).

trade. An example of this is a trade sanction. A sanction is generally the retaliatory reaction of a state against violations of international law by another state. Trade sanctions are also associated with the term retaliation, defined as a trade embargo is an example of a sanction and refers to state orders to prevent trade with a particular state. Basic variants of the trade embargo are the export embargo, the import embargo and the capital embargo.[74]

---

[74] Cf. Cavusgil, Knight and Riesenberger (2014, 212).

Barriers due to competition

Not only state-induced trade barriers but also competition in the target country can lead to market barriers. When analysing the resident competition in the target market, all significant existing competitors must be analysed. Porter divides competitors into four groups:

- (Still) Non-industry companies that can easily overcome the barriers to entry and thus become competitors.

- Companies that gain a strategic advantage by entering the industry.

- Non-industry companies for whom entering the industry would be an extension of their corporate strategy.

- (Potential) customers who can themselves become competitors and thus integrate into the industry.[75]

In order to restrict the choice of competition in practice, it is limited to undertakings offering directly competing products and services, and a comparison to this effect is therefore useful.[76]

However, data collection for competitor analysis is very complex and is divided into six groups, each with a different focus:

Group 1: Macroeconomic analysis,

Group 2: Business processes,

Group 3: Environmental analysis,

Group 4: Evolutionary factors,

Group 5: Financial factors,

---

[75] Cf. Porter (2014, 91).

[76] Cf. Porter (2014, 91f.).

Group 6: Complementary analysis.

Within the six groups there are many techniques for measuring the competitiveness of a company, of which the macroeconomic view in the immediate environment of the company is the most important part of the competition analysis.[77]

The competition can be divided into three basic groups. Some competitors can be identified directly, while others have an indirect influence.

1. The horizontal competitors are competitors who produce the same product or concentrate on the same customers. This group of competitors is the most direct and therefore most visible. An example for horizontal competitors is the car manufacturer Audi with the A6 and BMW with the 5 Series in the upper middle class.

---

[77] Cf. Fleisher and Bensoussan (2007, 83ff.).

2. The second is vertical competition. Here the companies compete for the same customers but come from two different sectors. These products can substitute each other. One example is the substitution of air travel with rail travel.

3. The last group is total competition. This type of competition is mainly present in the consumer goods market and includes all possible market participants from all sectors. Since the purchasing power of end consumers is limited and they have to make a purchasing decision, they are also in competition with these market participants.[78]

Once the competitors have been identified and the data collected in various ways, the actual analysis

---

[78] Cf. Berekoven, Eckert and Ellenrieder (2009, 298f.); Cf. Magerhans (2016, 265f.).

can be started by creating competitor profiles that cover the two different areas of hard and soft factors. Hard factors include facts and figures such as data on products, sales, legal forms, branches, number of employees or financial strength. The soft factors can include identifiable strategies, collaborations, quality/service and brand portfolios or images. These portfolios provide insight into the current situation and the position of competitors. In addition, these profiles can be compared with existing profiles from the past to identify any trends. The success story or the handling of failures also show how the competitors act and how they have dealt with such situations.[79] According to Aghazadeh, in order to analyse competition, it must be possible to assess the position of the company in the common market. The first and most important criteria used to

---

[79] Cf. Kerth, Asum and Stich (2015, 138).

assess the company's position are its market share and sales growth in the target market.[80]

[80] Cf. Aghazadeh (2016, 200).

Economic Barriers

Economic barriers can arise e.g. from operating cost advantages of established competitors. If an existing competitor has generated economies of scale based on experience, this leads to lower contribution margins and thus to cost disadvantages for a new entrant in the target market. A similar hurdle can arise if the established competitor has a particularly positive image in the market and considerable marketing efforts and thus high capital requirements are required for entry investments in order to gain a foothold in the foreign market. If, for example, a competitor has an outstanding position abroad, a high financial invest is necessary in order to build up a corresponding image for its own company. Especially when costly investments have to be made very specifically for a foreign market and are not relevant for other markets, this acts as a market barrier. In this case, the investments would be irretrievably lost in the event of failure on this market and would make it more difficult to exit the market, which would act as a barrier to entry because of the increased risk.[81]

Sometimes competitors deliberately build up economic barriers to entry by letting customers incur conversion costs if they want to switch to an alternative provider. Conversion costs can arise, for example, in the technological sector as well as in automation technology, as training costs are incurred for employees when a new technology is introduced. In such cases, newcomers must plan for considerably higher acquisition costs in order to make corresponding performance-related concessions to potential customers.

---

[81] Cf. Backhaus and Voeth (2010, 72f.).

Behavioural market barriers

Market entry barriers can also have behavioural causes. For example, customer loyalty towards domestic suppliers may make it more difficult for foreign suppliers to enter the market. For example, in the USA American light vehicle manufacturers still have the main market share. The biggest German car manufacturer holds only less than 4 per cent of the market share.

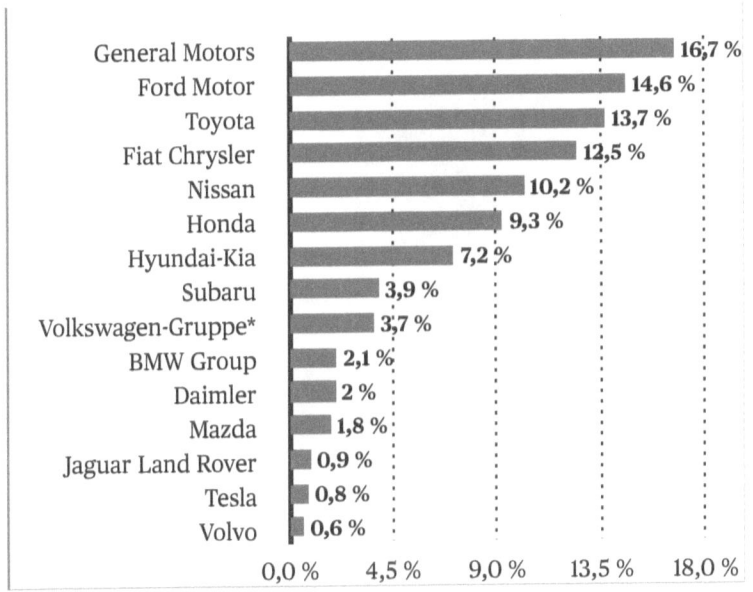

Figure 5.2: Market shares of automobile manufacturers in the USA[82]

In addition to loyalty barriers, difficulties in recruiting employees, language problems or cultural differences can play a role as a barrier to a supplier's market entry.

---

[82] GoodCarBadCar.net (2019).

Chapter 6 - National cultural barriers

The following chapter deals with the differences and influence of cultures on the activities of a company in an international environment. In the first step, the term culture is defined and an overview of the structure of cultures is given. Building on this, models are presented that attempt to analyse cultures and make them comparable.

There are numerous definitions of the term culture in the literature. Clifford Geertz describes culture as a pattern of inherited ideas and norms, expressed in symbolic form through which people communicate, preserve and develop their knowledge and attitudes towards life.[83] Culture is often associated with the concept of nation, but this is usually not the case. Within Britain, for example, there are several subcultures such as Scottish, English or Welsh. This means that cultures cannot always be reduced to national borders.[84] Basically, a culture can be divided into two levels. One level is perceptible to fellow human beings, whereas the other appears rather invisible. The invisible level of a culture includes, for

---

[83] Cf. Geertz (2006, 89).

[84] Cf. Sure (2017, 25).

example, basic assumptions, values, norms or attitudes. The visible level of a culture, on the other hand, is behavior and artefacts. These can be observed and seen and thus transform the invisible components of a culture into visible behaviours. A well-known metaphor in this context is that of the iceberg. According to this, the visible components are the tip of the iceberg that look out of the water. The invisible components form the foundation and thus the larger part that lies beneath the water.[85] This metaphor also illustrates the difficulty of dealing with cultures and why there are often mis-understandings and problems in cross-cultural cooperation. Edgar Schein writes in his book "Organisational Culture and Leadership" that one can only understand the visible actions of individuals if one knows the deep anchors, such as

---

[85] Cf. Kutschker (2011, 675).

traditional norms and values. This makes visible action easy to observe from his point of view, but difficult to decipher.[86]

For a long time, companies underestimated the effects of cultural differences and thus neglected to deal intensively with this topic. Only the strong internationalisation and the emerging problems in other countries brought the influence of national cultures into focus.[87]

In order to investigate and understand different cultures, there were a number of scientists who tried to compare them with the help of models and numbers. For this purpose, different categories are formed, which define typical behaviours and in which countries are classified. The following section briefly outlines two of these cultural models: Edward

---

[86] Cf. Schein (2010, 32).

[87] Cf. Kutschker (2011, 671f.).

Hall's and Fons Trompenaars'. They are intended to give an overview of the possibilities of analysing cultures.

Cultural differences according to Edward T. Hall

A model for the analysis of cultural differences and their effects on daily life is that of Hall. It divides a culture into four dimensions. The first is the fast vs. slow transfer of information. For example, Americans are very open-minded and reveal information about themselves more quickly, whereas Europeans tend to be more cautious. The second dimension is high context vs. low context. This dimension is about how much background information is needed by a conversation partner.[88] The third dimension is distance. This includes, for example, the physical distance between people.[89] The last dimension is polychronic and monochronic time orientation.

[88] Cf. Hall and Hall (2006, 6ff.).

[89] Cf. Hall and Hall (2006, 10f.).

These describe the sensation of time and how we deal with it.[90]

---

[90] Cf. Hall and Hall (2006, 13ff.).

Cultural Dimensions of Trompenaars

Another cultural model are the dimensions of Trompenaars. It comprises seven dimensions in three relationships and was strongly oriented towards the Hofstede model, which will be explained in detail in the next chapter. The first relationship is the relationship between people and includes points such as individualism vs. collectivism or achievement vs. origin. The second relationship describes the attitude to time. Trompenaars describes whether a culture is more past, present or future oriented. The latter describes the relationship to the environment. Some cultures try to control and influence the environment. Others, on the other hand, are more respectful of nature and respect their environment.[91]

In the following chapter the cultural dimensions of Geert Hofstede are presented and described in detail. It is regarded as one of the first models and is also based on one of the most extensive studies.

---

[91] Cf. Trompenaars and Hampden-Turner (2012, 10ff.).

Cultural dimensions according to Hofstede

Around 1970 Hofstede developed the concept for analysing the cultural differences between different countries. To make this possible, he evaluated data sets from a survey in which almost 50 foreign branches of IBM participated. The fact that all employees worked for the same company in almost the same positions allowed good conclusions to be drawn regarding cultural differences. The central reason for this is that their nationality was almost the only thing that distinguished them.[92] In order to make the different data comparable, Hofstede refers to the psychologist Daniel Levinson and the sociologist Alex Inkeles, who in an investigation recognised and identified

---

[92] Cf. Hofstede (1997, 13f.).

fundamental problems within societies worldwide. These are:

- The relationship to authority.

- Relationships between social and individual interests.

- The idea of the role of an individual in masculinity and femininity.

- The way you resolve conflicts and deal with your aggression and feelings.[93]

Hofstede then reformulated these four basic problems into so-called dimensions. In this case, dimensions represent an aspect of a culture that can be measured in relation to other cultures.

The Hofstede dimensions are power distance, collectivism vs. individualism, femininity vs. masculinity and uncertainty avoidance.[94] Over the

---

[93] Cf. Hofstede (1993, 28).

[94] Cf. Hofstede (1993, 29).

years, this concept has developed into one of the best-known cultural analyses in the economy.[95]

The following section describes the four original dimensions and the fifth, long-term orientation added in a later edition.

Power distance

The first dimension is the power distance. The power distance essentially describes the topics of structuring activities and centralising power and thus gives indications of the relationship between a superior and his employees.[96] If the value of power distance is high, it means that decision-making and power in a company is more centralised and distributed among a few employees. So, employees must mainly do what they are told and assigned to

---

[95] Cf. Schmitz and Weber (2014, 12).

[96] Cf. Hofstede (1980, 133).

do. In addition, there are clear hierarchical structures and several levels of power.[97]

With a low value in the range of the power distance, the employees see themselves rather equal with their boss. Decision making is not so centralised, but rather decentralised. Hierarchies are also flatter and there are not so many superordinate positions. In summary, managers in countries with a small power distance are more democratically oriented. The differences between the salaries of employees and bosses are smaller, and other privileges such as their own parking space or toilet are also limited. This is different in countries with a high-power distance. Here the ideal boss is rather an autocrat. Privileges and a special status are recognised and sometimes even desired.[98]

---

[97] Cf. Hofstede (1993, 50).

[98] Cf. Hofstede (1997, 37ff.).

Collectivism vs. individualism

The second dimension describes whether the focus is on individual or collective cultural interests. Hofstede describes that in a collectivist culture such as Singapore, the "we" feeling is at the forefront. This usually has family backgrounds. People often live not only with their immediate family, i.e. parents and siblings, but also with grandparents, uncles, aunts, etc. This leads to the fact that they see themselves as part of a larger group and regard other families as a different group. This creates a great loyalty to their own group as well as certain dependencies and a strong bond to them. An individualistic culture like most Nordic countries (Germany, Denmark, Sweden, etc.) is more "I" oriented. Here, too, the family plays the central role. Children often only live with their parents and siblings and grandparents and other family members are not seen as often. The children learn to orient themselves and to develop individually. This helps the individuals to quickly become independent and to leave their parents' house. It shows that they can take care of themselves and that there is no dependency on a group.[99]

In working life, this means that a manager in a collectivist culture leads a whole group, whereas in individually shaped countries, individuals represent different interests and must therefore be treated differently. Moreover, collectivist cultures are more focused on individuals than on the company. This means that a personal relationship between business partners must first be established before trust is gained and business can be conducted. In individually shaped countries, the focus is on the

[99] Cf. Hofstede (1997, 50f.).

task and the company, not on the personal relationship with the business partner.[100]

Geert Hofstede sees a negative correlation between these two dimensions. It can be observed that cultures with high power distances are more collectivist and countries with low power distances are more individualistic. The main reason for this is that in the we-groups there is usually a head of family who has a stronger position of power with much authority. In the case of individual families, on the other hand, all family members are regarded as having equal rights, which also means that they are not so dependent on powerful persons.[101]

Masculinity vs. femininity

The next dimension that Geert Hofstede has defined is the masculinity vs. the femininity of a culture. This

---

[100] Cf. Hofstede (1997, 66f.).

[101] Cf. Hofstede (1993, 28).

does not refer to biological differences, but to social and cultural differences. In other words, this dimension deals with whether the behavior of individual individuals is more determinant or restrained. Thus, women are more family-oriented and assume the soft, emotional roles. Men, on the other hand, are usually considered hard and performance/competitive. Points associated with Hofstede masculinity are, for example, salary as an opportunity to earn a lot or promotion to higher positions. Femininity is associated with points such as the relationship to superiors or employees, as well as a secure job.[102] Consequently, some central differences between masculine and feminine cultures can be identified. In feminine cultures, interpersonal relationships are important, modesty is expected, equality and solidarity are paramount in

---

[102] Cf. Hofstede (1993, 98f.).

working life, conflicts are discussed, and compromises are sought. In masculine cultures, however, money and objects play an important role. Employees must be hard, ambitious and decisive. This is why fairness and competition between colleagues prevail in working life. Performance must first be achieved, and conflicts are usually resolved.[103] So basically you can say that in masculine cultures it's about being the best at what you do, whereas in feminine cultures it's more about having fun at what you do.[104]

Uncertainty avoidance

The last of the four original dimensions is uncertainty avoidance. *„What is different, is dangerous "*[105] is one of the core statements of this

---

[103] Cf. Hofstede (1993, 115).

[104] Cf. Hofstede (2019).

[105] Hofstede (1997, 109).

dimension of Hofstede. It measures the extent to which people within a culture feel threatened by unknown, undefined or uncertain situations. For these people, such events express themselves in the form of stress or the need for predictability or rules. Furthermore, it is common in states with little uncertainty avoidance to keep aggressions and emotions to oneself. To show these is sometimes even socially despised. The opposite is the case with strong uncertainty avoidance. People tend to be restless, active or even aggressive. In spite of everything a strong uncertainty avoidance does not mean a risk avoidance. Rather it concerns here the unknown and undefined, because risks can be also well-known and therefore consciously taken.[106] This dimension also influences working and business life. In countries with high uncertainty avoidance,

---

[106] Cf. Hofstede (1993, 133ff.).

punctuality and accuracy are important characteristics and there is an inner urge for hard work. Motivation often comes from security needs or appreciation and there may even be resistance to new and innovative things. With low uncertainty avoidance the well-being has priority. Hard work is only done when it is necessary. Punctuality and accuracy must be learned, and people are open to new and innovative things.[107]

Short-term vs. long-term orientation

In 1991 Hofstede added a fifth dimension, short-term vs. long-term orientation. This was not present in the original version of the cultural dimensions, as the necessary questions were not part of the IBM study. A few years later, however, they were examined by the Chinese Value Survey and then included in the model by Hofstede. The basic idea of this dimension

---

[107] Cf. Hofstede (1993, 146).

is to find out whether long-term or short-term successes or goals are important for a culture.[108] More precisely, the long-term orientation expresses that people of this culture want to achieve their goals in the future with perseverance and thrift. Short-term oriented cultures, on the other hand, are more in the past or present and the aim is to achieve short-term goals in the near future. With regard to thrift, these cultures even feel a kind of social pressure to consume. They are also concerned about their status and social obligations. Long-term cultures, on the other hand, are willing to subordinate themselves to a particular task. A survey identified typical characteristics of an Asian (long-term) way of working. These are hard work, self-discipline, honesty or even responsibility. Short-term cultures (Americans) are somewhat more individual. Here,

---

[108] Cf. Hofstede, Hofstede and Minkov (2010, 239).

freedom of expression, individual rights, personal goals and thinking about oneself are in the foreground.[109] Furthermore, companies either attach more importance to increasing their profit within the next 10 years or they tend to think from year to year. Looking at the differences between personal relationships, it is important for long-term cultures to build and maintain long relationships and networks. In the dimension of short-term orientation, the opposite is true. Here the relationships change according to the benefits for the business.[110]

[109] Cf. Hofstede, Hofstede and Minkov (2010, 243ff.).

[110] Cf. Hofstede, Hofstede and Minkov (2010, 251).

Chapter 7 - Internationalisation strategies

In order to be successful in a market right from the start, a company must choose the right form of entry in order to take advantage of opportunities and minimise risks. Depending on the form of the market entry, however, some essential factors are influenced. These include the organisational structure, the degree of control over the foreign activities, the necessary know-how regarding the employees and the foreign market, the amount of investments to be made and thus also the risk a company takes. Nevertheless, companies have the opportunity to change their strategy at a later date after entering the market. However, this is often associated with considerable costs and time, which means that market entry strategies have gained considerable importance in the course of internationalisation.[111] If a company has already entered a market and changes its strategy in the following years, this is not a market entry, but a market cultivation.[112]

---

[111] Cf. Zentes (2012, 25f.).

[112] Cf. Kutschker (2011, 848).

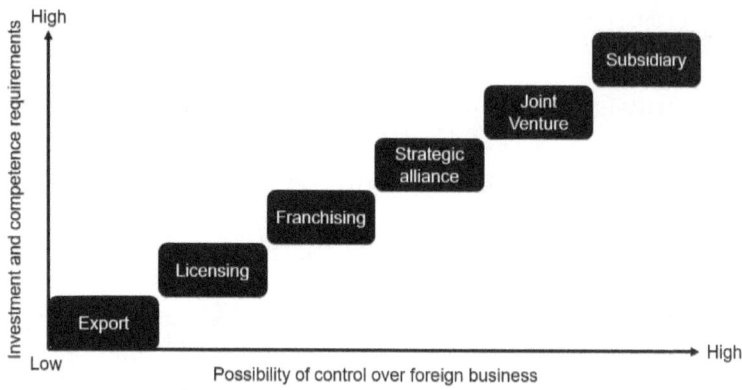

Figure 7.1: Stages of market entry[113]

The figure above shows the six basic stages of the various forms of market entry in terms of control and the level of investment and skills required. This means that market entry varies according to the type of entry in terms of the level of investment and competence requirements, but also the degree of control. Some of these six forms of entry can, however, be further subdivided on closer inspection.

---

[113] Own illustration according to Meffert, Burmann and Becker (2010, 176).

Export

Export is one of the most traditional forms of internationalisation of companies. This market entry strategy means the cross-border provision of economic services. A distinction is made between two types of export, indirect and direct export. In both cases, the value-added activity is largely on the domestic market and is not outsourced.[114]

In the case of indirect export, the company does not export directly abroad. Rather, it looks for a domestic intermediary who can locate customers in the target market and negotiate with them. In return, the sales agent receives a commission, which incurs additional costs for the company. In return, it does not have to deal with cultural differences between

---

[114] Cf. Zentes (2012, 28).

countries.[115] As a result, the competence requirements of the employees and the level of investment are very manageable. In addition, the company does not bear any risk because the agent buys the goods from the company and then exports them. On the other hand, the company does not gain any foreign experience in the event that it later wants to be directly active on the market.[116] In addition, the intermediary can also export products from the competition, which could create conflicts of interest and affect loyalty.[117]

The next figures illustrate both export forms in their processes. As can be seen, the company acts in the case of direct export without a domestic sales agent. In this case, the company can export to its own or

---

[115] Cf. Glowik (2016, 157).

[116] Cf. Meffert, Burmann and Becker (2010, 179f.).

[117] Cf. Glowik (2016, 157).

external distribution bodies abroad. Foreign distribution bodies can again be intermediaries, such as wholesalers or importers. Own distribution organs, on the other hand, would be, for example, sales or subsidiary companies. However, this form of export would mean a direct investment abroad.[118]

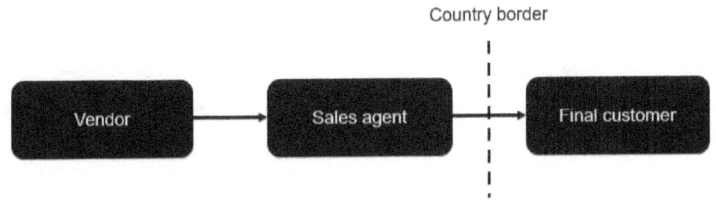

Figure 7.2: Indirect export[119]

Another alternative is direct sales without a sales agent from the head office to the customer. This results in increased travel costs and you have to negotiate the general conditions with the customer

[118] Cf. Meffert, Burmann and Becker (2010, 180).

[119] Own illustration according to Glowik (2016, 157) and Meffert, Burmann and Becker (2010, 179).

yourself. However, this also provides important information about the market and customers, which helps in the further course of internationalisation.[120]

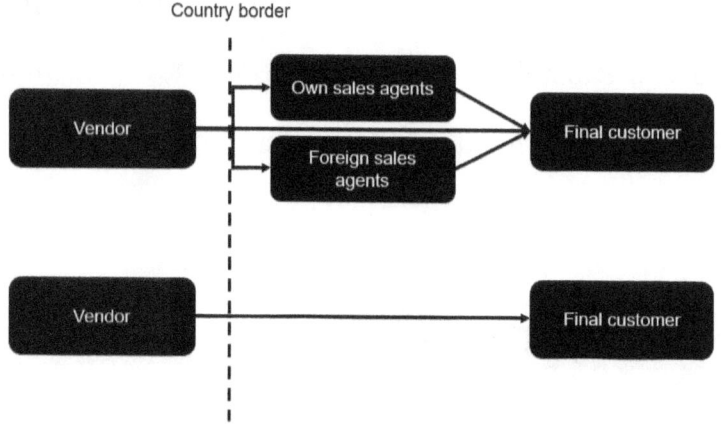

Figure 7.3: Direct export with and without sales agents in the foreign country[121]

---

[120] Cf. Glowik (2016, 157).

[121] Own illustration according to Glowik (2016, 157) and Meffert, Burmann and Becker (2010, 179).

114

Licensing and Franchising

Further market entry strategies are licensing and franchising. With these two forms, the focus of value creation is no longer on the domestic market, but on the respective market.[122] Licensing focuses on industrial goods, whereas franchising is mostly used in the service sector.[123]

Licensing and franchising are contractual agreements between a foreign contractor and a domestic contractor. They are very similar in structure, although there are some differences. In a licensing agreement, the contractor receives various assets such as patents, technical know-how or copyrights.[124] A distinction is made between

---

[122] Cf. Meffert, Burmann and Becker (2010, 176).

[123] Cf. Meffert, Burmann and Becker (2010, 181ff.).

[124] Cf. Kutschker (2011, 867ff.).

manufacturing licenses, distribution licenses and usage licenses. In return, the Contractor must pay license fees to the Contractor. These can be fixed amounts that are paid either periodically or once, or variable amounts that are based on turnover, sales or profit. For small to medium-sized companies, licensing their products is very advantageous because it is quite profitable on the one hand and requires few resources and investments on the other.[125]

On the negative side, the licensor has no control over the business and the quality of the product in the respective country. In addition, there are no learning effects or economies of scale.[126]

In franchising, the contractor performs certain activities and services using the brand and

---

[125] Cf. Meffert, Burmann and Becker (2010, 181).

[126] Cf. Glowik (2016, 165).

equipment of the contractor. As explained above, franchising focuses on services and distribution. As with licensing, incoming payments and variable payments are due based on turnover or profit.[127] The main advantages of a franchising concept are the synergies that can be achieved. The contracting party controls its know-how in the areas of research & development (R&D), marketing and management and can thus also achieve better economies of scale. In return, the contractor abroad has the necessary regional market experience and cultural sensitivity to optimally market the product.[128]

Here, too, the risk is very low for the franchisor, as he does not make high investments. On the other hand, the disadvantage is that the franchisor has no influence on the local business. This can damage the

---

[127] Cf. Meffert, Burmann and Becker (2010, 183).

[128] Cf. Glowik (2016, 166).

good reputation if the franchisee does not act in the best interests of the company. In addition, it limits the profit potential, as the franchisee does not skim off the full market, but only receives the entry payment and the variable payments.[129]

---

[129] Cf. Kutschker (2011, 880).

Joint Venture and strategic alliance

Further market entry strategies are cooperation on the foreign market through joint ventures or strategic alliances. At least two independent companies join forces to achieve a specific goal. The main difference is that in a joint venture a legally independent company is set up and thus a capital transfer of the participating companies takes place. In a strategic alliance, on the other hand, there are often more than two companies involved and, in addition, there is usually no need to set up a new entity with equity participation.[130]

Joint ventures are particularly useful when you are entering markets that have high entry barriers or import bans. With a local partner you can avoid these problems and comply with the guidelines.

[130] Cf. Meffert, Burmann and Becker (2010, 185f.).

Cooperation with other companies can bring advantages for both cooperative market entry strategies. For example, you can learn from your partners and gain new knowledge. At the same time, the rivalry in a market decreases because potential competitors work together. Costs can also be reduced by benefiting from economies of scale. On the other hand, both forms also have disadvantages. These can be, for example, the loss of know-how or the need for a high level of communicative coordination with the partners. In addition, mutual trust and thus the right choice of partner are necessary in order to operate successfully in the market.[131]

---

[131] Cf. Kutschker (2011, 891ff.).

Subsidiary

The last and therefore most intensive form of entry with regard to the investment and competence requirements and the degree of control is the establishment of a subsidiary. This can be done in two ways. On the one hand, a new foreign company can be established (so-called greenfield investments) or an existing company can be purchased. Both ways make it possible to operate directly on the market and to have maximum control over foreign business. In addition, profits do not have to be shared. A negative aspect is that you have to bear losses yourself, which significantly increases the risk.[132]

An acquisition can be either vertical or horizontal. This means that you can acquire a competitor

---

[132] Cf. Zentes (2012, 27).

(horizontally) or buy a trading company or a producer (vertically). Irrespective of this, the company definitely acquires competencies and resources. On the other hand, problems may arise in bringing together the different corporate cultures. Acquisitions are usually very costly, so they are rarely used by Small and Medium Enterprises (SMEs).[133]

The problem of merging corporate cultures does not play a role in a start-up, but the start-up has some disadvantages. For example, there is a need to look more closely at national culture. In addition, the rivalry within the market is increased, it is very time-consuming to establish oneself and personnel are needed.[134]

---

[133] Cf. Meffert, Burmann and Becker (2010, 188f.).

[134] Cf. Kutschker (2011, 911f.).

Summary and critical examination

In the third chapter of this paper, methods for assigning market typologies to countries were presented. In addition, typical internationalisation strategies are listed that can be linked to market typologies later in this paper.

However, a comprehensive overview cannot be given in the context of this paper. The consideration of risk, for example, is completely omitted or is only briefly addressed within the framework of market barriers. The market situation can be judged in a wrong way or the reputation of the competitors because of the big part of subjective criteria - how this affects the internationalisation strategy is not clear. In addition, the influence of the deployment of foreign new employees on the corporate culture or the danger posed by employee espionage are not considered at all. Overall, therefore, change management and the risks associated with it are not addressed.

In addition, it is questionable how practicable the methods described here really are. Can a reliable assessment be made for all the criteria presented on the basis of publicly available indicators or empirical analyses? This will be presented in the next section - but the author cannot give an outlook on the basis of the theoretical approaches presented.

During the development of the theoretical approaches within the last part of this chapter, the author focused on national cultural differences as they play an important role in the work of international teams. This approach is particularly critical. Despite the many awards and recognition, some scientists are critical of Hofstede's model. Especially Professor Brendan McSweeney criticised his model. The main point of criticism was that the model does not deal with the individual differences within a culture, but rather regards the entire nation as homogeneous, without considering the diversity of people.[135]

Hansen also criticised this and stated that the results of his work would have been completely different if he had questioned the executive floor instead of the lower and middle ranks of the IBM hierarchy. Or he would have chosen students or artists. In doing so, he accuses Hofstede of generalising a sub collective and seeing it as an umbrella collective for the entire nation.[136]

However, there is no other model that contains these points, nor is there any model that so characterises the theme of cultural differences. The criticism of

---

[135] Cf. McSweeney (2002, 110f.).

[136] Cf. Hansen (2009, 15).

the model can be used to summarise that the models presented only give a rough overview of the different differences. It seems almost impossible to define each culture precisely and to define a guideline for dealing with them. There are too many subcultures and other influences such as the status within a society.

Chapter 8 - How to enter the Central and Eastern Europe countries?

In the previous chapter, methods were shown for classifying markets into market typologies. The determination of the market attractiveness and the market barriers are of decisive importance here.

In the following chapter, the classification of the initially defined target markets in Central and Eastern Europe into market typologies is carried out in full. First, the diagram of market attractiveness and market barriers is labeled with numerical values in order to provide quantitative evidence of their classification into market typologies. Subsequently, a weighting of all criteria described in the previous chapters is carried out. Subsequently, the quantitative evaluation of all criteria is carried out.

At the end of this chapter, an evaluation of the results is carried out with the selection of a suitable internationalisation strategy for each of the CEEC8 countries, also summing up the results of the evaluation of all criteria for each country.

Empirical classification of the CEEC8 countries in market typologies with the survey method

As already described in the introduction of this elaboration, a classification of the CEEC8 states into market typologies is carried out within the framework of this section. For this purpose, the empirical research method of the survey is used. While a completely structured questionnaire is used for quantitative surveys, qualitative surveys use a guideline that contains a list of key questions as well as a list of topic groups that need to be addressed.[137]

For the classification of the CEEC8 countries into market typologies, a total of three different surveys are carried out, with which on the one hand the weighting of the criteria and on the other hand the

---

[137] Cf. Lang (2019, 6).

qualitative and quantitative evaluation are carried out (see appendix).

The surveys have been distributed in German language to a total of 247 people, coming from different companies in Germany. All potential participants are employed in an industrial environment and come from the fields of development, application, sales, purchasing or human resources and must have access to international companies. All respondents were able to answer the survey either in full or in part. A total of 539 responses were received, distributed in different ways across the three survey pages.

In the first survey, the weighting of the main criteria explained in the third section is asked directly. The survey participants determine how important (from extremely unimportant to extremely important) the main criteria are to them when setting up a commercial agency abroad (see appendix).

In the second survey, the weighting of the sub-criteria also explained in the previous section is indirectly determined. The participants in the survey receive a thesis for each criterion, which you can either not agree at all or completely agree with (see appendix).

The third survey is aimed at all criteria that can only be determined qualitatively and therefore, from the author's point of view, cannot be determined by public indicators. Here the participants of the survey vote on in which of the countries the qualitatively determinable conditions for establishing a commercial agency are most likely to be fulfilled (see appendix).

Scaling the Market Attractiveness Market Barrier Diagram

For a classification on the basis of quantitative data into the market typology diagram to take place, the qualitative terms "low" and "high" must first be replaced by numerical values (see figure 8.1).

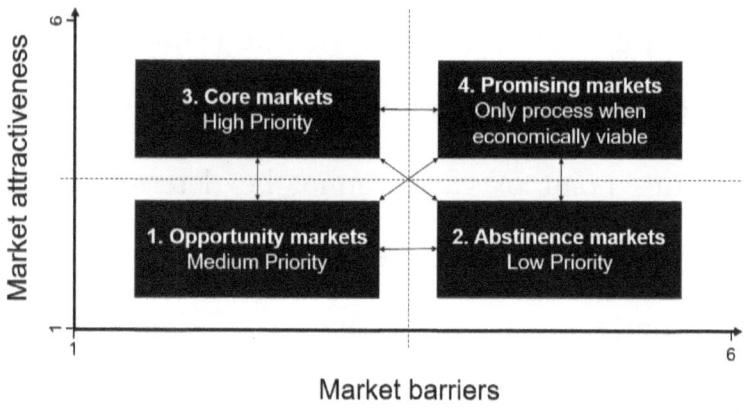

Figure 8.1: Scaled diagram of market typologies[138]

---

[138] Extended illustration by the author according to Backhaus and Voeth (2010, 71).

In order to eliminate the "urge to the middle", an even number of selection options for the rating scale is offered here, as already described in the third chapter of this paper. [139]

The author has decided to use a scale of 1 to 6 to evaluate the criteria. In contrast to the German school grading system, however, here one stands for the lowest possible value (worst rating or lowest degree of fulfilment) and six for the highest possible value (best rating or highest degree of fulfilment).

In relation to the classification of the CEEC8 countries in the scaled market typology diagram, this means that the CEEC8 countries are included in the scaled market typology diagram:

The market is regarded as an opportunity market if the market barriers are rated between 1 and 3.5 and

---

[139] Cf. Helm (2009, 217ff.).

the attractiveness of the market is rated between 1 and 3.5.

The market is regarded as abstinence market if the market barriers are rated between 3.5 and 6 and the market attractiveness is rated between 1 and 3.5.

The market is considered a core market if the market barriers are rated between 1 and 3.5 and the market attractiveness between 3.5 and 6.

The market is regarded as a promising market if the market barriers are rated between 3.5 and 6 and the market attractiveness is rated between 3.5 and 6.

Calculation of market attractiveness with the scoring method

As described in the chapter before the market attractiveness and market barriers will be calculated with the scoring method. Therefore, different criteria are considered with weighted scoring values.

Table 8.1: Scoring criteria for market attractiveness

Market attractiveness	Chapter 3.2			1,00
Production cost advantages	Chapter 3.2.1	20,00%		1,00
Demand-related advantages	Chapter 3.2.2	20,00%		1,00
Competitive advantages	Chapter 3.2.3	20,00%		1,00
Internationalization advantages	Chapter 3.2.4	20,00%		1,00
Digital competitiveness	Chapter 3.2.5	20,00%		1,00

The criteria for determining market attractiveness consist of all the components described in the previous chapters. These are production cost advantages, demand-related advantages, competitive advantages, internationalisation advantages and digital competitiveness. The overall evaluation of the market attractiveness is carried out by the sum of the individual evaluations, which are multiplied in each case by your weighting.

In the overview presented in Table 8.1, no weighting of the criteria has yet been carried out. This will be included in the evaluation of the empirical data later in the following section.

Calculation of market barriers with the scoring method

T he assessment of market barriers is carried out in the same way as the assessment of market attractiveness.

Table 8.2: Scoring criteria for market barriers

Market barriers	Chapter 3.3			1,00
Tariff barriers	Chapter 3.3.1	20,00%		1,00
Competition barriers	Chapter 3.3.2	20,00%		1,00
Economic barriers	Chapter 3.3.3	20,00%		1,00
Behavioral market barriers	Chapter 3.3.4	20,00%		1,00
Cultural barriers	Chapter 3.3.5	20,00%		1,00

The criteria for determining the market barriers consist of all components described in the previous sections. These are tariff barriers competition barriers, economic barriers, behavioural market barriers and cultural barriers. The overall evaluation of the market barriers is also carried in the same way as the evaluation of the market attractiveness.

In the overview presented in Table 8.2, no weighting of the criteria has yet been carried out as well. This will also be included in the following section.

Chapter 9 - Determination of the market attractiveness of the CEEC8 countries

This section extracts the criteria for determining market attractiveness from the third chapter. Each criterion is assigned its own weighting in order to be able to apply it to the scoring procedure. This weighting is derived from an empirical survey[140] (see appendix).

The weighting in percent for each criterion is determined as follows:

1. The arithmetic mean of the result of the evaluation is taken from survey 1 for the main criterion. The arithmetic mean of all subordinate criteria is taken from survey 2.

2. The sum of all arithmetic mean values of the survey results belonging to the main criterion results in the necessary score for a 100% rating.

3. In order to obtain the weighting of the individual criterion, the first named value and the second named value are divided.

---

[140] All survey results can be downloaded at https://www.umfrageonline.com/results/65a96c4-0b7ecf7 or achieved from the appendix of this elaboration

Within the main part of this elaboration the survey-results are shown and also the resulting weighting.

Following the weighting of each criterion, the evaluation method, which can be either qualitatively subjective or quantitatively objective, is also determined by the author. With the help of publicly available indicators or empirical studies, an evaluation between 1 and 6 can be assigned to each criterion following this section. Each criterion is assigned through a calculation to scale the survey-results that they fit in the 1 to 6 scale. The calculation method for all criteria are presented in the appendix.

Production cost advantages

As described in the previous chapter the production cost advantages are weighted as follows:

Table 9.1: Weighting of production cost advantages

	Survey result (average)	Resulting weighting
Production cost advantaged	4,09	17,97%
Labor costs	2,80	25,23%
Working hours	2,80	25,23%
Supply of raw materials	2,40	21,62%
Prices for raw materials	3,10	27,93%

With a resulting weighting of 17.97%, the production cost advantages have the least influence on the question of whether to set up a branch abroad. The weighting of the criteria, on the other hand, is uniform.

The evaluation of the labor costs criterion is determined on the basis of the minimum wage in the country. The lower the minimum wage the better the rating. Labor costs in Europe are taken from the Hans-Böckler-Stiftung[141] .

Table 9.2: Rating of labor costs

	CZ	SK	SL	HU	LT	PL	BU	RO
Minimum wage / €	3,11	2,99	**5,1**	2,69	3,39	3,05	**1,72**	2,68
Rating	3,94	4,12	**1,00**	4,57	3,53	4,03	**6,00**	4,58

The evaluation of the working hours can be done with consideration of the mean working time per week in the country. The more working hours the better the rating. Therefore, EUROSTAT made a study in 2017[142] .

---

[141] Hans-Böckler-Stiftung (2019).

[142] EUROSTAT (2017).

Table 9.3: Rating of working hours

	CZ	SK	SL	HU	LT	PL	BU	RO
Mean working hours per week	41,7	41,2	41,4	40,6	**39,8**	**41,9**	41,1	40,3
Rating	5,53	4,34	4,81	2,91	**1,00**	**6,00**	4,10	2,19

The rating of the supply of raw materials can only be done in a qualitative way. Therefore, the survey 3 (see appendix) is used.

Table 9.4: Rating of supply of raw materials

	CZ	SK	SL	HU	LT	PL	BU	RO
Result of survey 3	**3**	**0**	**0**	**0**	1	1	**0**	**0**
Rating	**6,00**	**1,00**	**1,00**	**1,00**	2,67	2,67	**1,00**	**1,00**

Prices of raw materials are evaluated in the same way as the supply of raw materials, shown in the table above.

Table 9.5: Rating of prices of raw materials

	CZ	SK	SL	HU	LT	PL	BU	RO
Result of survey 3	0	0	0	0	3	0	1	2
Rating	1,00	1,00	1,00	1,00	6,00	1,00	2,67	4,33

Demand-related advantages

The following table shows the survey results on demand-related advantages:

Table 9.6: Weighting of demand-related advantages

	Survey result (average)	Resulting weighting
Demand-related advantages	5,25	23,07%
Number of potential customers	5,50	24,44%
Market growth	4,50	20,00%
Market structure	4,60	20,44%
Country-specific purchasing power	3,50	15,56%
Price sensitivity of the buyer groups	4,40	19,56%

The survey's top rating of 23.07% makes clear that demand-related advantages are of the highest importance when deciding to invest abroad. When weighting the criteria, it is noticeable that the number of potential customers is particularly important.

The number of potential customers for companies in the Automation technology sector is in direct proportion to the turnover created in the machine building sector. Therefore, the author collected data from EUROSTAT (see appendix)[143].

Table 9.7: Rating of number of potential customers

	CZ	SK	SL	HU	LT	PL	BU	RO
Turnover in machine building 2018 / Mill. €	**12764,8**	5146,13	1624,05	6877,37	**133,92**	10542,5	1058,03	3686,69
Rating	**6,00**	3,01	1,60	3,70	**1,00**	5,16	1,37	2,42

Market growth is evaluated through the growth of turnover in machine building between the last actual

---

[143] EUROSTAT (2018).

values from 2018 compared with estimated values from 2023 from EUROSTAT[144].

Table 9.8: Rating of market growth

	CZ	SK	SL	HU	LT	PL	BU	RO
Turnover growth '18 to '23 / Mill. €	608	**952**	128	545	36	**1**	110	545
Rating	4,22	**6,00**	1,68	3,89	1,19	**1,00**	1,58	3,88

The market structure is a qualitative criterion. The rating is done through survey 3 (see appendix).

Table 9.9: Rating of market structure

	CZ	SK	SL	HU	LT	PL	BU	RO
Market structure	4	0	0	0	1	2	0	0
Rating	6,00	1,00	1,00	1,00	2,25	3,5	1,00	1,00

---

[144] EUROSTAT (2018).

The gross domestic product (GDP) is an indicator for the economic growth of the purchasing power of a country. The GDP is a measure of the economic performance of an economy over a given period. It measures the value of goods and services produced in the economy (value added), as they are not used as intermediate consumption for the production of other goods and services.[145] The higher the GDP the better the rating of the country-specific purchasing power. Therefore, data from IZA is used[146].

Table 9.10: Rating of country-specific purchasing power

	CZ	SK	SL	HU	LT	PL	BU	RO
GDP / €	19400	16600	**22200**	13500	16100	12900	**7800**	10400
Rating	4,11	3,27	**6,00**	2,34	3,12	2,16	**1,00**	1,41

---

[145] Cf. Statistisches Bundesamt (2019).

[146] IZA Institute of Labor Economics (2019, 5).

The price sensitivity of the buyer groups is evaluated qualitatively with survey 3 (see appendix).

Table 9.11: Rating of price sensitivity of the buyer groups

	CZ	SK	SL	HU	LT	PL	BU	RO
Result of survey 3	0	0	2	0	1	1	0	0
Rating	1,00	1,00	6,00	1,00	3,5	3,5	1,00	1,00

Competitive advantages

The following table shows the survey results on the competitive advantages.

In comparison to the other criteria, the weighting of competitive advantages is lower with 22.41%.

Technological superiority is measured through the results of survey 3 (see appendix).

Table 9.13: Rating of technological superiority

	CZ	SK	SL	HU	LT	PL	BU	RO
Result of survey 3	5	0	0	0	1	1	0	0
Rating	6,00	1,00	1,00	1,00	2	2	1,00	1,00

The rating of the own market strength and the number of competitors has to be analysed for your own company here to complete the analysis.

The rating of the market access criterion is done qualitatively with the expert survey, made with survey 3 (see appendix).

Table 9.14: Rating of market access

	CZ	SK	SL	HU	LT	PL	BU	RO
Market-access	1	0	0	0	1	2	0	1
Rating	3,5	1,00	1,00	1,00	3,5	6	1	3,5

As the reversibility can be considered quantitatively e.g. through the price of factory buildings, human resource costs and machine costs within this elaboration only the rent index is taken into consideration[147] .

---

[147] NUMBEO (2019).

Table 9.15: Rating of reversibility

	CZ	SK	SL	HU	LT	PL	BU	RO
Rent index compared to GER/ %	**-28,7**	-41,5	-41,6	-48,8	-52,5	-43,2	**-65,3**	-62,4
Rating	**1,00**	2,74	2,75	3,75	4,25	2,97	**6,00**	5,60

As all CEEC8 countries are following the regulations by the European Union the conditions of competition are on the most attractive level. Therefore, all countries will get the top rating.

Table 9.16: Rating of conditions of competition (state-regulation)

	CZ	SK	SL	HU	LT	PL	BU	RO
Conditions of competition (state-regulation)	0	0	0	0	0	0	0	0
Rating	6,00	6,00	6,00	6,00	6,00	6,00	6,00	6,00

Internationalisation advantages

How important the internationalisation advantages are to the participants in the survey is shown below:

Table 9.17: Weighting of internationalisation advantages

	Survey result (average)	R e s u l t i n g weighting
Internationalization advantages	4,17	18,39%
Optimization of logistics	4,10	51,90%
International supply of skilled workers	3,80	48,10%

As in general the optimisation of logistics the shorter the delivery time is, and the less money is necessary to ship a package to the customer the better the logistics are. As all CEEC8 countries are supported by DHL express delivery service in the same way as sending packages within Germany, the founding of a subsidiary does not optimise the delivery time at all[148]. In addition, transport with an intermediate stop e.g. in a sales office, where additional administration is required, is generally more expensive than direct delivery. Therefore, the rating is set to the minimum value for all CEEC8 countries.

Table 9.18: Rating of optimisation of logistics

	CZ	SK	SL	HU	LT	PL	BU	RO
Optimizati on of logistics	0	0	0	0	0	0	0	0
Rating	1,00	1,00	1,00	1,00	1,00	1,00	1,00	1,00

The international supply of skilled workers can only be evaluated in a qualitative way through an expert's survey (see appendix). Therefore, survey 3 is used.

---

[148] DHL (2019).

Table 9.19: Rating of international supply of skilled workers

	CZ	SK	SL	HU	LT	PL	BU	RO
Result of survey 3	3	0	0	0	3	1	0	0
Rating	6,00	1,00	1,00	1,00	6,00	2,67	1,00	1,00

Digital competitiveness

Digital competitiveness has also been weighted below:

Table 9.20: Weighting of the digital competitiveness

	Survey result (average)	Resulting weighting
Digital competitiveness	4,17	18,39%
Knowledge	3,60	30,77%
Technology	3,90	33,33%
Future readiness	4,20	35,90%

In the digital competitiveness studies for all countries ratings between 0% and 100% exist[149]. Knowledge, Technology and Future readiness are taken into consideration with that approach.

---

[149] Cf. IMD WORLD COMPETITIVENESS CENTER (2018, 54ff.).

Table 9.21: Rating of knowledge, technology and future readiness

	CZ	SK	SL	HU	LT	PL	BU	RO
Knowledge	38	49	26	48	23	33	41	45
Rating	2,90	3,45	2,30	3,40	2,15	2,65	3,05	3,25
Technology	31	47	38	40	30	37	42	44
Rating	2,55	3,35	2,90	3,00	2,50	2,85	3,10	3,20
Future readiness	34	53	35	58	33	37	55	57
Rating	2,70	3,65	2,75	3,90	2,65	2,85	3,75	3,85

Chapter 10 - Determination of the market barriers of the CEEC8 countries

In this section, the criteria for identifying market barriers are extracted from the third chapter in a similar way as for market attractiveness. Each criterion is assigned its own weighting in order to be able to apply it to the scoring procedure. Just as in the calculation of market attractiveness, the overall assessment of market barriers results from the sub-summation of several individual criteria, which can be either qualitatively subjective or quantitatively objective. With the help of publicly available indicators or empirical studies, each criterion also can be assigned a rating between 1 and 6 following this section. The higher the rating of the criteria, the higher the barrier.

The calculation method follows the same procedure as for determining market attractiveness (see appendix).

Tariff barriers

Table 10.1: Weighting of tariff barriers

	Survey result (average)	Resulting weighting
Tariff barriers	5,17	21,60
Quantitative restrictions for exports of goods	4,10	29,71%
Laws and regulations against international trade	5,00	36,23%
Buy local campaigns	4,70	34,06%

As all CEEC8 countries follow European trade laws, there are no tariff barriers at all. Therefore, the resulting ratings are at the lowest possible value.

Table 10.2: Rating of quantitative restrictions for exports of goods, laws and regulations against international trade and buy local campaigns

	CZ	SK	SL	HU	LT	PL	BU	RO
Quantitative restrictions for exports of goods	0	0	0	0	0	0	0	0
Rating	1,00	1,00	1,00	1,00	1,00	1,00	1,00	1,00
Laws and regulations against international trade	0	0	0	0	0	0	0	0
Rating	1,00	1,00	1,00	1,00	1,00	1,00	1,00	1,00
Buy local campaigns	0	0	0	0	0	0	0	0
Rating	1,00	1,00	1,00	1,00	1,00	1,00	1,00	1,00

Competition barriers

The strength of horizontal competition can be measured through the number of competitors who are already active in the target market. This has to be done for your company and market you want to analyse individually. In table 10.3 the number of vendors for automation technology has been counted by the author of this elaboration.

Table 10.3: Rating of strength of horizontal competition

	CZ	SK	SL	HU	LT	PL	BU	RO
Active horizontal competitors in target country	4	2	4	4	3	4	3	3
Rating	6,00	1,00	6,00	6,00	3,5	6,00	3,5	3,5

Classical vertical competition practically does not take place in automation technology in which in times of industry 4.0 all suppliers are forced to deliver solutions instead of products only. The same applies to total competition. For this reason, the resulting barrier is evaluated with the minimum value.

Table 10.4: Rating of vertical competition and total competition

	CZ	SK	SL	HU	LT	PL	BU	RO
Strength of vertical competition	0	0	0	0	0	0	0	0
Rating	1,00	1,00	1,00	1,00	1,00	1,00	1,00	1,00
Strength of total competition	0	0	0	0	0	0	0	0
Rating	1,00	1,00	1,00	1,00	1,00	1,00	1,00	1,00

Economic barriers

Table 10.5: Weighting of economic barriers

	Survey result (average)	Resulting weighting
Economic barriers	4,75	19,85%
Operating cost advantages of established competitors	4,90	37,69%
Necessary marketing invests abroad	3,80	29,23%
Conversion cost barriers by established competitors	4,30	33,08%

Operating cost advantages, influenced by economics of scale effects, are not taken into consideration for sales subsidiaries at all but for subsidiaries with an own assembly or production line in the automation technology sector. Thus, the assessment of this criterion is based on the number of producing competitors abroad as presented in the previous sections of this elaboration.

Table 10.6: Rating of operating cost advantages of established competitors

	CZ	SK	SL	HU	LT	PL	BU	RO
Number of producing competitors	1	1	4	2	1	2	1	2
Rating	1,00	1,00	6,00	2,67	1,00	2,67	1,00	2,67

To find quantitative values to rate the necessary marketing invest abroad a study by Philipp Roth and Jens Wiese is used. Roth and Wiese collected the price for advertisements on Facebook in all European countries[150]. As the most expensive advertisements on Facebook are in Switzerland with a value of 0,48€ the CEEC8 countries' rating is compared with this value.

---

[150] Roth and Wiese (2011).

Table 10.7: Rating of the necessary marketing invest abroad

	CZ	SK	SL	HU	LT	PL	BU	RO
Facebook ad. Costs / €	0,22	<0,12	<0,12	<0,12	<0,12	<0,12	<0,12	<0,12
Rating	3,29	2,25	2,25	2,25	2,25	2,25	2,25	2,25

In order to be able to evaluate the conversion cost barriers by established competitors, an indicator is necessary to determine the conversion costs of automation technology. For this the author uses a study of the Fraunhofer Institute. In this study on the machine tool industry, the distribution of the life cycle costs of a machine tool assumes the major part of over 37% of the total costs in maintenance and inspection, which also includes the use of automation technology.[151] The author makes the assumption that a change of supplier of automation

---

[151] Cf. Mattes and Schröter (2012).

technology is tantamount to a complete overhaul of the machine, resulting in the same costs as for inspection and maintenance over the entire lifetime. This value is the same for the whole branch, valid for all CEEC8 countries.

Table 10.8: Rating of conversion cost barriers by established competitors

	CZ	SK	SL	HU	LT	PL	BU	RO
Lifecycle costs at supplier change	37%	37%	37%	37%	37%	37%	37%	37%
Rating	6,00	6,00	6,00	6,00	6,00	6,00	6,00	6,00

Behavioural barriers

Table 10.9: Weighting of behavioural barriers

	Survey result (average)	Resulting weighting
Behavioral market barriers	4,92	20,56%
Loyalty towards domestic suppliers	4,30	30,94%
Language barrier	4,70	33,81%
Recruiting possibility	4,90	35,25%

B ehavioural market barriers can only be taken into consideration from qualitative values. Therefore, survey 3 results are considered (see appendix.)

Table 10.10: Rating of loyalty towards domestic suppliers

	CZ	SK	SL	HU	LT	PL	BU	RO
Result of survey 3	0,00	0,00	0,00	3,00	1,00	1,00	0,00	0,00
Rating	1,00	1,00	1,00	6,00	2,67	2,67	1,00	1,00

Table 10.11: Rating of language barrier

	CZ	SK	SL	HU	LT	PL	BU	RO
Result of survey 3	0,00	1,00	0,00	2,00	0,00	0,00	0,00	3,00
Rating	1,00	2,67	1,00	4,33	1,00	1,00	1,00	6,00

Table 10.12: Rating of recruiting possibility

	CZ	SK	SL	HU	LT	PL	BU	RO
Result of survey 3	0,00	0,00	0,00	3,00	0,00	1,00	0,00	0,00
Rating	1,00	1,00	1,00	6,00	1,00	2,67	1,00	1,00

Cultural barriers

According to Hofstede's' cultural dimensions approach all five dimensions should have the same weight. Therefore, the author decided not to take a change of the weighting of the cultural dimensions into consideration.

Table 10.13: Weighting of cultural barriers

	Survey result (average)	Resulting weighting
Cultural barriers	4,17	17,43%
Power distance	-	20,00%
Collectivism vs. Individualism	-	20,00%
Femininity vs. Masculinity	-	20,00%
Uncertainty avoidance	-	20,00%
Long-term orientation	-	20,00%

The assessment of the cultural dimensions is carried out by comparing the respective dimensional characteristics of the country with those in Germany. The greater the difference of the dimension compared to the German value is the bigger the rating for the cultural barrier is. A value of 1 is assigned when the difference equals 0. A value of 6 is assigned for the biggest difference in the data series.

Table 10.14: Rating of power distance

	CZ	SK	SL	HU	LT	PL	BU	RO	DE
Power Distance	57	**100**	71	46	42	68	70	90	**35**
Difference to Germany	22	**65**	36	11	7	33	35	55	**0**
Rating	2,69	**6,00**	3,77	1,85	1,54	3,54	3,69	5,23	**1,00**

Table 10.15: Rating of individualism

	CZ	SK	SL	HU	LT	PL	BU	RO	DE
Individualism	58	52	**27**	80	60	60	30	30	**67**
Difference to Germany	9	15	**40**	13	7	7	37	37	**0**
Rating	2,15	2,92	**6,00**	2,66	1,90	1,90	5,74	5,74	**1,00**

Table 10.16: Rating of masculinity

	CZ	SK	SL	HU	LT	PL	BU	RO	DE
Masculinity	57	100	**19**	88	19	64	40	42	**66**
Difference to Germany	9	34	**47**	22	47	2	26	24	**0**
Rating	1,96	4,62	**6,00**	3,34	6,00	1,21	3,77	3,55	**1,00**

Table 10.17: Rating of uncertainly avoidance

	CZ	SK	SL	HU	LT	PL	BU	RO	DE
Uncertainly avoidance	74	51	88	82	**65**	**93**	85	90	**65**
Difference to Germany	9	14	23	17	**0**	**28**	20	25	**0**
Rating	2,61	3,50	5,11	4,04	**1,00**	**6,00**	4,57	5,47	**1,00**

Table 10.18: Rating of long-term orientation

	CZ	SK	SL	HU	LT	PL	BU	RO	DE
Long-term Orientation	70	77	49	58	82	**38**	69	52	**83**
Difference to Germany	13	6	34	25	1	**45**	14	31	**0**
Rating	2,44	1,67	4,78	3,78	1,11	**6,00**	2,56	4,44	**1,00**

Chapter 11 - Definition of the internationalisation strategy for the CEEC8 countries

---

In the following section, the author uses the empirically determined results of the market attractiveness and market barriers for each of the CEEC8 countries to develop an internationalisation strategy made for a company which is acting in the automation technology sector.

First, within the Market Attractiveness Market Barrier Diagram, one or more possible internationalisation strategies are defined for each of the four quadrants which contain market typologies. This is followed by a country-by-country assessment supported by additional literature sources with additional information

Assignment of internationalisation strategies to market typologies

In the previous chapters possible internationalisation strategies have already been named and their advantages and disadvantages described. If the market typology is known, not all internationalisation strategies are automatically recommended. From the explanations in the third chapter, the author now makes recommendations for the best internationalisation strategy for the respective market typology.

Figure 11.1: Internationalisation strategies for different market typologies

1. Opportunity markets are characterised by the fact that market attractiveness is relatively low, but market barriers do not make market entry too difficult. The aim of the market entry strategy is to create a market entry with the lowest possible investment sum. Strategic control does not play an important role here.

For these reasons, franchising and licensing of industrial contractual partners and system integrators are particularly suitable as market entry strategies.

2. Abstinence markets are characterised by high market barriers and low market attractiveness. Therefore, market cultivation should only take place with low priority. Sales responds to the few inquiries received from the market, but an investment abroad should not be made.

For these reasons, the internationalisation strategy of direct export is recommended.

3. Core markets have a comparatively high market attractiveness with comparatively low market barriers, which leads to a particularly high priority of market cultivation. Entry into a core market should therefore be characterised by the highest possible strategic control. A high investment sum in the core market can easily be justified by rising revenues and thus profit repatriations.

For these reasons, the author recommends working on core markets exclusively with subsidiaries in the country.

4. Promising markets have relatively high market barriers but are nevertheless characterised by relatively high market attractiveness. The aim of the selected internationalisation strategy is to keep the risk of high market barriers as low as possible while exploiting the high potential of the market as fully as possible.

For this reason, the joint venture and strategic alliance market entry strategies are particularly suitable.

Internationalisation approaches for the CEEC8 countries

From the empirical analysis of this paper, the market attractiveness and market barriers of all CEEC8 countries can be evaluated and drawn in a common table:

Table 11.1: Market attractiveness and market barriers of the CEEC8 countries

	CZ	SK	SL	HU	LT	PL	BU	RO
Market barriers	2,09	2,01	2,89	3,20	1,94	2,62	2,14	2,76
Market attractiveness	3,56	2,64	2,22	2,35	2,95	2,91	2,43	2,63
Market typology	3.	1.	1.	1.	1.	1.	1.	1.

From these collected values for market attractiveness and market barriers, a diagram can be created for classification into market typologies.

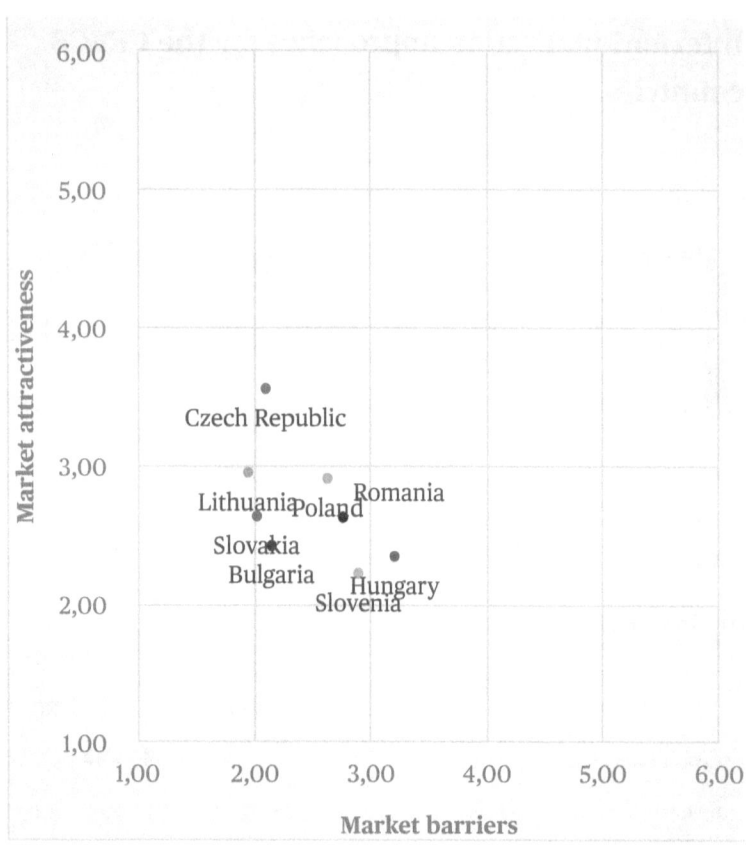

Figure 11.2: Market typologies of the CEEC8 countries

Internationalisation approach for the Czech Republic

In the last 10 years, since the economic crisis, investors benefited from the country's stable political and economic environment in Czech Republic because of the above-average pace of its transition process, as well as its geographic proximity to EU markets. Nevertheless, the Czech Republic showed a relatively reserved attitude towards foreign direct investments during the initial stage of its transition, investors soon found their way to the country.[152]

There are already over 500 start-ups in the Czech Republic. Prague is developing into a leading center for innovative start-ups in Central Eastern Europe. The young, fast-growing technology companies

---

[152] Cf. Szent-Iványi (2017, 51).

usually focus on global markets right from the start. They are finding more and more private investors to invest in start-ups. Even German companies are now benefiting from Czech venture capital.

The technical and digital focus is striking in the product range of the growth companies. The majority of start-ups offer outsourcing of software and IT infrastructure, web services, mobile software services or cloud technologies. Current industrial topics such as Nano- and biotechnology, new materials or photonics play only a minor role. Two thirds of start-ups have developed an innovative product. The rest imitate existing ideas or adapt them. Every third start-up has its own patents or registered trademarks.[153]

For these reasons, the Czech Republic has been able to prove itself as a core market in this elaboration as

---

[153] Cf. GTAI (2017, 6).

well. The internationalisation strategy clearly is to set up a subsidiary in the Czech Republic in order to counter this emerging market with a worthwhile investment that will help exploit the market potential.

Internationalisation approach for Slovakia

After more than ten years of economic stagnation and political isolation, Slovakia reappeared on the maps of multinational corporations and emerged as one of the prime destinations for foreign direct investments in Europe. Major investors, such as Kia, PSA (Peugeot and Citroën) and Samsung, flocked into the country and influenced Slovakia a lot.[154]

The Slovak government has adopted a concept for the development of intelligent production. It is thus responding to the challenges of industry 4.0. The plan is to keep the strong industrial base in the country and make it fit for the future through the use of digital technologies. However, the starting conditions are not particularly rosy. Compared to

---

[154] Cf. Szent-Iványi (2017, 77f.).

other economies in the region, Slovakia is lagging behind.[155]

The author's conclusion for the internationalisation strategy of Slovakia, which has turned out to be an opportunity market within this elaboration, is franchising or licensing of industrial partners in Slovakia.

---

[155] Cf. GTAI (2017, 10).

Internationalisation approach for Slovenia

The Slovenian economy is one of the fastest growing in the European Union (EU). Gross domestic product (GDP) grew by 4.9 and 4.5 percent in 2017 and 2018, respectively, about twice as fast as the EU as a whole (2.5 and 2 percent). According to EU Commission forecasts, GDP growth will slow in 2019 and 2020, but will remain above the EU average.[156]

During this elaboration Slovenia proved to be one of the countries within the CEEC8 countries with the highest market barriers and relatively low market attractiveness. The internationalisation strategy is again franchising or licensing of local sales partners.

---

[156] Cf. GTAI (2019).

Internationalisation approach for Poland

Polish industry wants to increase its innovative strength and is investing in automation technology - both in devices and programs. Around 600 robots are purchased every year, mainly from the automotive industry. Cloud solutions are gaining in importance in the software sector, not least because of the cost advantage. However, cost-benefit comparison is ultimately the biggest obstacle for industry 4.0 in Poland: a robot is worth four times less than in Germany.[157]

With three third highest ratings for market attractiveness after Lithuania and the Czech Republic, Poland is also characterised by below-average market barriers in comparison with the

---

[157] Cf. GTAI (2017, 8).

other CEEC8 countries. As a result, Poland is clearly positioned within the opportunity markets and is scratching the border to the core markets. Here it is therefore advisable to initially enter the market through franchising or licensing, which can, however, be extended to the establishment of a subsidiary if the market attractiveness continues to grow over the next few years.

Internationalisation approach for Hungary

With the highest valuation for market barriers and a relatively low value for market attractiveness, Hungary is only just in the area of opportunity markets. Although the internationalisation strategy is therefore also licensing or franchising, it should first concentrate on the other countries of the CEEC8 states before planning internationalisation beyond direct export towards Hungary.

Internationalisation approach for Bulgaria

The Bulgarian economy grew by 3.3% in 2018, but the industrial sector only grew by 0.8%, partly due to the shortage of labor. The projects planned for the EU funding period 2014-2020 finally started in 2018 (motorway and underground construction) and stimulated domestic demand. In 2018, the Bulgarian trade balance was again more in deficit (-2.2 billion euros), export growth slowed to 3.2% and imports rose by 6.3% due to higher domestic demand. In the World Bank report "Doing Business 2019", which compares parameters for business activity in 190 countries, Bulgaria fell 9 places to 59th place. Bulgaria's weakest performance was in connection to the electricity grid, payment of taxes and insolvency proceedings.[158]

The classification of Bulgaria in the Market Barriers Market Attractiveness Diagram as Opportunity Market also leads to franchising and licensing as internationalisation strategies.

---

[158] Cf. AußenwirtschaftsCenter Sofia (May 2019, 3ff.).

Internationalisation approach for Lithuania

In the Baltic States, the market volume for machinery and equipment totals more than 1.9 billion euros. Agricultural and forestry machinery is the largest product category. The shortage of skilled workers due to emigration and rising wages are leading to increasing pressure for automation. In addition to similarities, the markets in Estonia, Latvia and Lithuania have specific characteristics which make them attractive for Automation technology companies.[159]

---

[159] Cf. GTAI (2017, 12).

Table 11.2: Major machine builders and plant constructors in the Baltic States[160]

OEM	Branch	Turnover 2015 in million Euro
Axis Industries (Lithuania)	Plant constructor	128,0
Hekotek AS (Estonia)	Woodworking machinery, Intralogistics	54,7
Umega AB (Lithuania)	Ovens, agricultural and forestry machinery	22,9
Tech Group AS (Estonia)	Automation of production plants	9,2
Transportation Technology Systems SIA (Latvia)	Intralogistics	9,0
Rikon AS (Latvia)	Intralogistics	6,0

Within this elaboration Lithuania proved to be the CEEC8 country with the second highest market attractiveness rating after the Czech Republic. The

---

[160] GTAI (2017, 12).

market barriers are rated even lower than the Czech Republic. From these valuations, Lithuania is classified as an opportunity market, but in a similar way to Poland also in perspective with a change to the core market. The resulting internationalisation strategy is therefore initially franchising or licensing, but in perspective the establishment of a subsidiary in Lithuania can also be a worthwhile investment.

Internationalisation approach for Romania

Romania, with its assessment of market attractiveness and market barriers, is in the midfield of the analysed CEEC8 countries and in the midfield of the opportunity markets. The low-risk internationalisation strategy of franchising or licensing is also recommended for Romania.

Summary and critical questioning of the results of the empirical study

In the fourth section of this paper, the methods from the third section were verified within a scoring procedure using publicly available key figures and, in part, empirically determined survey results. The results are polarising and provide clear recommendations for action as soon as the presented theoretical approaches are linked by the author: The selection of an internationalisation strategy on the basis of market typology does not take place in this way in the literature used - this is an independent work of the author and makes the results obtained in this way questionable. In contrast to this are the polarising results, which can lead to clear recommendations for action.

When carrying out the scoring procedure, the empirical evaluation of some criteria must be viewed particularly critically. In the case of small sample sizes, the result is not representative of the broad masses but merely forms the opinion of a small group. This means that the empirically determined criteria are nevertheless more resilient than those from an expert interview, for example.

When looking at the results, the relatively high ranking of Lithuania as a worthwhile country for foreign direct investment is particularly surprising, which may be due to the above-mentioned critical view.

Chapter 12 - Conclusion

The aim of this paper was to develop an internationalisation strategy for automation technology companies in Central and Eastern Europe. For this purpose, empirical data were collected for all countries of the CEEC8 states, which enable the classification of the states into market typologies through the evaluation of market attractiveness and market barriers. For all CEEC8 countries an internationalisation strategy could be defined, whereby the goal of this elaboration is fulfilled.

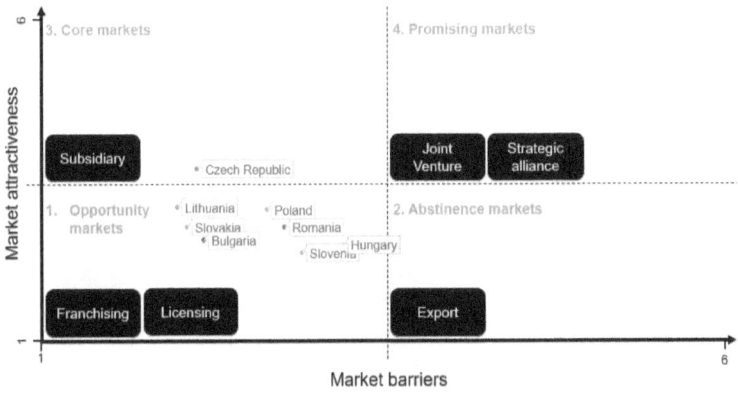

Figure 12.1: Internationalisation approaches for the CEEC8 countries

In the classification of CEEC8, the Czech Republic in particular as a core market is out of the picture. All other countries are opportunity markets in which a lower-risk investment is worthwhile. The main reason for this is primarily the low average value of market barriers due to the fact that the CEEC8 states belong to the European Union.

The development of the industrial machine building market in Central and Eastern Europe is particularly worthwhile for European suppliers. For an automation technology supplier the priority of market development is highest in the Czech Republic followed by Lithuania and Poland.

Appendix

Please download the full appendix at:

https://drive.google.com/drive/folders/11y5OLThYprav3y5laloEX-dcOlGKQO5n?usp=sharing

References

Aghazadeh, Hashem (2016): Principles of marketology, volume 1: Theory. New York, s.l.: Palgrave Macmillan US.

AußenwirtschaftsCenter Sofia (2019): Wirtschaftsbericht Bulgarien. Available at https://www.wko.at/service/aussenwirtschaft/bulgarien-wirtschaftsbericht.pdf. Publication date May 2019, accessed 28.07.2019.

Backhaus, Klaus (2003): Industriegütermarketing. 7th ed. München: Vahlen (Vahlens Handbücher der Wirtschafts- und Sozialwissenschaften.

Backhaus, Klaus; Voeth, Markus (2010): Internationales Marketing. 6th ed. Stuttgart: Schäffer-Poeschel.

Baiba Grandovska; Michele Marotta (2019): Euro area international trade in goods. Publication date Februar 2019, accessed 01.05.2019.

Bain, Joe S. (1956): Barriers to New Competition: Their Character and Consequences in Manufacturing Industries. s.l.: Harvard University Press (Harvard University Series on Competition in American Industry: 3).

Bea, Franz Xaver; Haas, Jürgen (2017): Strategisches Management. 9th ed. Konstanz, München: UVK Verlagsgesellschaft mbH; UVK/Lucius (UTB Betriebswirtschaftslehre: 8498).

Berekoven, Ludwig; Eckert, Werner; Ellenrieder, Peter (2009): Marktforschung: Methodische Grundlagen und praktische Anwendung. 12th ed. Wiesbaden: Gabler Verlag / GWV Fachverlage GmbH Wiesbaden.

Berndt, Ralph; Fantapié Altobelli, Claudia; Sander, Matthias: Internationales Marketing-Management. 5th ed. (SpringerLink Bücher.

Biesel, Hartmut H. (2013): Vertriebsarbeit leicht gemacht: Die besten Strategiewerkzeuge, Checklisten und Lösungsmuster. 2nd ed. Wiesbaden: Springer Gabler (SpringerLink.

Bundesanzeiger, Festo AG & Co. KG (2018): Umsatz der Festo AG & Co. KG in den Jahren 2010 bis 2017

(in Milliarden Euro). Available at https://
de.statista.com/statistik/daten/studie/444500/
umfrage/umsatz-von-festo/. Publication date 2018,
accessed 03.06.2019.

Büschemann, Karl-Heinz (2013): Pleite nach
Lehrbuch: Gescheiterte Fusion von Daimler und
Chrysler. Süddeutsche Zeitung. Available at https://
www.sueddeutsche.de/wirtschaft/gescheiterte-
fusion-von-daimler-und-chrysler-pleite-nach-
lehrbuch-1.1666592-0. Publication date 07.05.2013,
accessed 11.08.2019.

C.K. Prahalad; Venkat Ramaswamy (2004): C-
Creation Experiences: The Next Practice in Value
Creation. In: *Journal of Interactrive Marketing,* 2004
(3), 5-15. Available at https://deepblue.lib.umich.edu/
bitstream/handle/2027.42/35225/20015_ftp.pdf,
accessed 11.06.2019.

Cavusgil, S. Tamer; Knight, Gary A.; Riesenberger, John R. (2014): International business: The new realities. 3rd ed. Boston: Pearson.

Cynthia A. Montgomery; Michael E. Porter (1991): Strategy: Seeking and Securing Competitive Advantage. Publication date 1991.

DHL (2019): PREISE INTERNATIONAL: Versandkosten für Ihren weltweiten Versand. Available at www.dhl.de, accessed 20.07.2019.

Dunning, John H.; Lundan, Sarianna M. (2008): Multinational enterprises and the global economy. 2nd ed. Cheltenham: Elgar.

Eichele, Richard (2019): Markteintrittsstrategien für Zentral- und Osteuropa: Masterarbeit Gewichtung Kriterien. Available at https:// www.umfrageonline.com/results/65a96c4-0b7ecf7. Publication date 18.07.2019, accessed 18.07.2019.

Ernst, Dietmar (1999): Internationalisierung kleiner und mittlerer Unternehmen: Kooperationsformen und Außenwirtschaftsförderung. Wiesbaden, s.l.: Deutscher Universitätsverlag (Gabler Edition Wissenschaft.

European Commission (2019): EU IN 2018;GENERAL REPORT ON THE ACTIVITIES OF THE EUROPEAN UNION. [S.l.]: EUROPEAN COMMISSION.

EUROSTAT (2017): Durchschnittliche Wochenarbeitszeit von Vollzeitbeschäftigten in den Ländern der Europäischen Union (EU-28) im Jahr 2017 (in Stunden). Available at https://de.statista.com/statistik/daten/studie/75864/umfrage/durchschnittliche-wochenarbeitszeit-in-den-laendern-der-eu/, accessed 20.07.2019.

EUROSTAT (2018): Wholesales trade turnover in [country] 2011-2023. Available at https://

de.statista.com/marktprognosen, accessed 10.05.2019.

Fleisher, Craig S.; Bensoussan, Babette E. (2007): Business and competitive analysis: Effective application of new and classic methods. Upper Saddle River, NJ: Financial Times Press.

Geertz, Clifford (2006): The interpretation of cultures: Selected essays. New York: Basic Books (Basic book-s.

German Electrical and Electronic Manufacturers' Association (2019): Electric Industry in Numbers: The Electric Industry in Germany. Abteilung Wirtschaftspolitik, Konjunktur und Märkte (April 2019). Available at https://www.zvei.org/fileadmin/user_upload/Presse_und_Medien/Publikationen/2019/Maerz/Elektroindustrie_in_Zahlen_2019/ZVEI_Elektroindustrie_in_Zahlen_2019.pdf. Publication date April 2019, accessed 01.06.2019.

Glowik, Mario (2016): Market Entry Strategies: Internationalization Theories, Concepts and Cases of Asian High-Technology Firms: Haier, Hon Hai Precision, Lenovo, LG Electronics, Panasonic, Samsung, Sharp, Sony, TCL, Xiaomi. 2nd ed. Berlin/ Boston: De Gruyter (De Gruyter Textbook.

GoodCarBadCar.net (2019): Market shares of selected automobile manufacturers in the USA in 2019*: share of light vehicle sales. Available at https:// de.statista.com/statistik/daten/studie/249338/ umfrage/marktanteile-der-automobilhersteller-in-den-usa/, accessed 10.06.2019.

Grunwald, Guido; Hempelmann, Bernd (2017): Angewandte Marketinganalyse: Praxisbezogene Konzepte und Methoden zur betrieblichen Entscheidungsunterstützung. Berlin, Boston: De Gruyter.

GTAI (2017): Mittel- und Osteuropa: Industrien im Wandeö. GTAI. Available at www.gtai.de. Publication date 2017, accessed 01.06.2019.

GTAI (2019): Wirtschaftsausblick - Slowenien (Mai 2019). Available at https://www.gtai.de/GTAI/ Navigation/DE/Trade/Maerkte/Wirtschaftsklima/ wirtschaftsausblick,t=wirtschaftsausblick--slowenien-mai-2019,did=2318192.html, accessed 28.07.2019.

Hall, Edward Twitchell; Hall, Mildred Reed (2006): Understanding cultural differences: Germans, French and Americans. Yarmouth, Me.: Intercultural Press.

Hans-Böckler-Stiftung (2019): WSI-Mindestlohnbericht 2019. Available at https:// de.statista.com/statistik/daten/studie/37401/umfrage/ gesetzliche-mindestloehne-in-der-eu/, accessed 20.07.2019.

Hansen, Klaus P. (2009): Die Problematik des Pauschalurteils. In: *interculture journal: Online Zeitschrift für interkulturelle Studien,* (8), 5-18. Available at http://www.interculture-journal.com/index.php/icj/issue/archive, accessed 14.06.2019.

Helm, Roland (2009): Strategische Analyse und marktorientierte Umsetzung. 8th ed. Stuttgart: Lucius & Lucius (Grundwissen der Ökonomik: 919).

Hofstede, Geert (1980): Culture's consequences: Cross-cultural research and methodology series. Beverly Hills: Sage Publ.

Hofstede, Geert (1993): Interkulturelle Zusammenarbeit: Kulturen - Organisationen - Management. Wiesbaden: Gabler.

Hofstede, Geert (1997): Cultures and organizations: Software of the mind ; [intercultural cooperation and its importance for survival. New York: McGraw-Hill.

Hofstede, Geert (2019): Hofstede Insights: Consulting | Training | Certification | Tooling. Available at https://www.hofstede-insights.com/, accessed 14.06.2019.

Hofstede, Geert; Hofstede, Gert Jan; Minkov, Michael (2010): Cultures and organizations: Software of the mind : intercultural cooperation and its importance for survival. New York: McGraw-Hill.

IMD WORLD COMPETITIVENESS CENTER (2018): IMD WORLD COMPETITIVENESS RANKING 2018. In: *IMD WORLD DIGITAL COMPETITIVENESS RANKING*, 2018, 1-177, accessed 10.05.2019.

IZA Institute of Labor Economics (2019): The Past and Future of Manufacturing in Central and Eastern Europe: Ready for Industry 4.0? In: *DISCUSSION PAPER SERIES*, 2019 (12141), 1-41, accessed 10.05.2019.

Kerth, Klaus; Asum, Heiko; Stich, Volker (2015): Die besten Strategietools in der Praxis: Welche Werkzeuge brauche ich wann? ; Wie wende ich sie an? ; Wo liegen die Grenzen? 6th ed. München: Hanser.

Koch, Eckart (2017): Globalisierung: Wirtschaft und Politik: Chancen - Risiken - Antworten. 2nd ed. Wiesbaden: Springer Gabler.

Kutschker, Michael (2011): Internationales Management. s.l.: Oldenbourg Wissenschaftsverlag.

Lang, Sabine (2019): Empirische Forschungsmethoden. Available at https://www.uni-trier.de/fileadmin/fb1/prof/PAD/SP2/Allgemein/Lang_Skript_komplett.pdf. Publication date 2019, accessed 18.07.2019.

Larry O'Brien; Craig Resnick; Allen Avery (2018): Top 50 Automation Companies of 2017: Digitalization takes over: The IIoT is transforming the Top 50 into software and services companies. Control Global. Available at https://www.controlglobal.com/articles/ 2018/top-50-automation-companies-of-2017- digitalization-takes-over/?stage=Live. Publication date 22.10.2018, accessed 01.06.2019.

Lutz Sommer (2009): Degree Of Internationalization: A Multidimensional Challenge. In: *The Journal of Applied Business Research*, 2009 (25), 93-110.

Magerhans, Alexander (2016): Marktforschung: Eine praxisorientierte Einführung. Wiesbaden: Springer Gabler.

Mattes, Katharina; Schröter, Marcus (2012): Wirtschaftlichkeitsbewertung: Bewertung der wirtschaftlichen Potenziale von energieeffizienten Anlagen und Maschinen: Kurzstudie. In: *Effizienzfabrik - Innovationsplattform Ressourceneffizienz in der Produktion*, 2012, 1-25.

Available at http://publica.fraunhofer.de/documents/
N-207035.html, accessed 20.07.2019.

McDonald, John (1996): Strategy in poker, business &
war. New York, London: Norton & Company.

McSweeney, Brendan (2002): Hofstede's Model of
National Cultural Differences and their
Consequences: A Triumph of Faith - a Failure of
Analysis. In: *Human Relations,* 55 (1), 89-118.
doi: 10.1177/0018726702551004.

Meffert, Heribert; Burmann, Christoph; Becker,
Christian (2010): Internationales Marketing-
Management: Ein markenorientierter Ansatz. 4th ed.
Stuttgart: Kohlhammer (Kohlhammer Edition
Marketing.

Meffert, Heribert; Burmann, Christoph; Kirchgeorg,
Manfred (2015): Marketing: Grundlagen
marktorientierter Unternehmensführung ; Konzepte

- Instrumente - Praxisbeispiele. 12th ed. Wiesbaden: Springer Gabler.

Michael E. Porter (1990): The Competitive Advantage of Nations. Harvard College (March-April). Available at http://www.economie.ens.fr/IMG/pdf/ porter_1990_- _the_competitive_advantage_of_nations.pdf. Publication date 1990, accessed 09.06.2019.

Moak, Ken (2017): Developed Nations and the Economic Impact of Globalization. Cham, s.l.: Springer International Publishing.

Morschett, Dirk; Schramm-Klein, Hanna; Zentes, Joachim (2015): Strategic international management: Text and cases. 3rd ed. Wiesbaden, s.l.: Springer Fachmedien Wiesbaden.

Mühlbacher, Hans; Leihs, Helmuth; Dahringer, Lee (2006): International marketing: A global perspective. 3rd ed. London: Thomson Learning.

NUMBEO (2019): Cost of Living. Available at www.numbeo.com, accessed 20.07.2019.

Perlitz, Manfred; Schrank, Randolf (2013): Internationales Management. 6th ed. Konstanz: UVK Verl.-Ges (Unternehmensführung: 8481).

Peter Altmaier (2018): Internationalen Handel stärken und Barrieren abbauen: Deutschland ist seit vielen Jahren eines der führenden Länder beim weltweiten Austausch von Waren und Dienstleistungen. Ein freier Welthandel mit fairen internationalen Wettbewerbsbedingungen gibt wichtige Impulse für Wirtschaftswachstum und Beschäftigung. Das BMWi setzt sich deshalb für offene Märkte mit klaren Regeln ein.

Porter, Michael E. (2014): Wettbewerbsvorteile: Spitzenleistungen erreichen und behaupten = (Competitive Advantage). 8th ed. Frankfurt am Main, New York: Campus Verlag (Campus Strategie.

Roth, Philipp; Wiese, Jens (2011): Facebook Werbepreise und Nutzerzahlen in Europa. Available at https://allfacebook.de/wp-content/uploads/2011/11/facebook_werbepreise_europa.pdf, accessed 20.07.2019.

Schein, Edgar H. (2010): Organizational culture and leadership. 4th ed. San Francisco, Calif.: Jossey-Bass (The Jossey-Bass business & management series.

Schmitz, Lena; Weber, Wiebke (2014): Sind die Hofsted'schen Kulturdimensionen valide?: Ein Messäquivalenztest der Hofsted'schen Unsicherheitsvermeidungsdimensionen. In: *interculture journal: Online Zeitschrift für interkulturelle Studien,* (13), 11-26, accessed 14.06.2019.

Siemens AG (2018): Siemens stattet ungarische Bahnlinie mit ETCS-Technologie aus. Available at https://www.siemens.com/press/de/

pressemitteilungen/index.php?
content%5B%5D=Corp&content%5B%5D=GP&conten
t%5B%5D=PGGT&content%5B%5D=PGDG&content%
5B%5D=PGSU&content%5B%5D=PGCP&content%5B
%5D=PGES&content%5B%5D=PGIE&content%5B%5D
=SI&content%5B%5D=DI&content%5B%5D=MO&cont
ent%5B%5D=MOMM&content%5B%5D=MOTPE&cont
ent%5B%5D=MOMLT&content%5B%5D=MOUT&cont
ent%5B%5D=MOCS&content%5B%5D=SFS&content%
5B%5D=SRE&content%5B%5D=PoC&search=Osteuro
pa&date-1-dd=03&date-1-
mm=06&date-1=2016&date-2-dd=03&date-2-
mm=06&date-2=2019&intern=1. Publication date
09.05.2018, accessed 03.06.2019.

Siemens AG (2019a): Annual Report 2018. Available
at https://assets.new.siemens.com/siemens/assets/
public.1552038192.4bfbab10-00d6-4a22-aad2-

b50f3f232bfb.siemens-annual-report-2018.pdf. Publication date 2019, accessed 01.06.2019.

Siemens AG (2019b): One global ambition. Available at https://new.siemens.com/global/en/company/jobs/ our-locations/location-pages.html. Publication date 03.06.2019.

SIMON-KUCHER & PARNTER (2005): Internationale Lenker, nationale Kontrolleure: Eine Untersuchung der Internationalität von Vorstand und Aufsichtsrat der DAX-Unternehmen. SIMON-KUCHER & PARNTER. Available at www.simon-kucher.com. Publication date 2005.

Statistisches Bundesamt (2019): Bruttoinlandsprodukt (BIP): Was beschreibt der Indikator? Available at https://www.destatis.de/DE/ Themen/Wirtschaft/Volkswirtschaftliche-Gesamtrechnungen-Inlandsprodukt/Methoden/ bip.html, accessed 10.05.2019.

Stephen Herbert Hymer (1960): The International Operations of National Firms: A Study of Direct Foreign Investment. Massachusetts Institute of Technology. Available at http://hdl.handle.net/1721.1/27375. Publication date June, 1960, accessed 04.06.2019.

Sudarsanam, Sudi (2009): Creating value from mergers and acquisitions: The challenges ; an integrated and international perspective. Harlow: Prentice Hall/Financial Times.

Sure, Matthias (2017): Internationales Management: Grundlagen, Strategien und Konzepte. Wiesbaden: Springer Gabler.

Swoboda, Bernhard (2002): Arbeitsbuch Marketing-Management. Stuttgart: Schäffer-Poeschel.

Szent-Iványi, Balázs (Ed.) (2017): Foreign direct investment in Central and Eastern Europe: Post-crisis perspectives. Cham: Palgrave Macmillan (Studies in economic transition.

Trompenaars, Fons; Hampden-Turner, Charles (2012): Riding the waves of culture: Understanding diversity in global business. 3rd ed. New York: McGraw-Hill.

UNCTAD (2008): Transnationality index of host economies. UNCTAD. Available at https://unctad.org/Sections/dite_dir/docs/wir2008_transnationality_chart_en.xls. Publication date 23.09.2008, accessed 11.05.2019.

UNCTAD (2019): Statistics: Transnationality Index. Available at https://unctad.org/en/Pages/statistics.aspx, accessed 11.05.2019.

Weizsäcker, C. C. (1980): Barriers to Entry: A Theoretical Treatment. Berlin, Heidelberg: Springer (Lecture Notes in Economics and Mathematical Systems: 185).

Welch, Lawrence S.; Benito, Gabriel R. G.; Petersen, Bent (2007): Foreign operation methods: Theory, analysis, strategy. Cheltenham, UK: Edward Elgar.

Westermann, Georg; Finger, Sabine (2012): Kosten-Nutzen-Analyse: Einführung und Fallstudien. Berlin: E. Schmidt (ESV basics.

Wiesner, Knut (2005): Internationales Management. München: Oldenbourg (WiSorium - Wirtschafts- und Sozialwissenschaftliches Repetitorium.

World Trade Organization (2019): Understanding the WTO: The Organization: Members and Observers. World Trade Organization. Available at www.wto.org. Publication date 29.07.2019, accessed 01.05.2019.

Zardari, Noorul Hassan; Ammed, Kamal; Shirazi, Sharif Moniruzzaman; Yusop, Zulkifli Bin (2015): Weighting methods and their effects on multi-criteria decision making model outcomes in water resources management. Cham, Heidelberg: Springer (Springer briefs in water science and technology.

Zentes, Joachim (2012): Markteintrittsstrategien: Dynamik und Komplexität. Wiesbaden: Gabler Verlag (mir-Edition.